THE RADICAL KINGDOM

The Radical Kingdom

NIGEL WRIGHT

KINGSWAY PUBLICATIONS
EASTBOURNE

First published 1986

ISBN 0 86065 399 4

Front cover design by Vic Mitchell

Printed in Great Britain for
KINGSWAY PUBLICATIONS LTD
Lottbridge Drove, Eastbourne, E. Sussex BN23 6NT by
Richard Clay (The Chaucer Press) Ltd, Bungay, Suffolk.
Typeset by CST, Eastbourne, E. Sussex.

With love and gratitude
to my parents
Muriel Wright and
Charles Somerville Wright, MBE

Contents

INTRODUCTION

Restoration in Theory and Practice

To use the word 'radical' in a positive way would once have been unthinkable among 'conservative' evangelicals. Radicals were beyond the pale. They were dangerous people whose theology owed more to current trends and philosophies than to Scripture. Added to that they would almost always take up a critical stance in relation to the received order and since most theological conservatives appear also to be socially conservative, the threat was compounded. Radicals were to be identified with communists and worse. But a new phenomenon has emerged among evangelical people. Perhaps it would be truer to say that it has re-emerged. A deep vein of Christian radicalism is beginning to find expression and it comes from different quarters.

Evangelicals are now in the forefront of those who use the word 'radical' and who believe that it aptly describes what God is calling them to be. There are those in the so-called, but misnamed, 'house-church movement' who have passed through the experience of renewal and have come to the conclusion that God requires radical obedience of those who honour Jesus as Lord and that this obedience impinges directly upon the nature and form of our life together in the church. Renewal of the individual Christian leads to reformation of the corporate believers. The church should look again, therefore, at its patterns and structures, its practices and its performance and should let God judge them. It should look again at its roots and should assess itself in the light of Scripture. It should then have the courage to break free from futile ways inherited from the past and should be the church Christ envisaged.

There are others who are advocates of 'radical discipleship' and who relate the need for us to return to our roots not so much to the structures of our church life as to our ethical stance within the world. The church is being called to rediscover the ethic of Jesus who presented the kingdom of God not as a programme of social conservatism but as a force which confronted and contradicted the powers of his day. Specifically this has to do with the stance Christians take to wealth, to vested interest, to the poor and to violence. We are, according to the advocates of this position, too easily and too completely fashioned in the image of this world. While being particular about remaining pure and undefiled in small things, we capitulate wholesale in the weightier matters and we are compromised. We need to become radically obedient whatever it costs us.

This book is an attempt at synthesis. It is written by one who is seeking to live by the principles it contains. It is not a manual of how to do it as if the Christian pilgrimage could be reduced to easy formulae, but it is an attempt to wrestle with the issues. It is not a scholarly book but it does come out of an attempt to think. The issues touched on in this book do not arise out of books so much as out of life. It is the product of a struggle—not yet anywhere complete—to be responsive to some of the issues being raised by the Holy Spirit in the church today and to work out how they apply to a band of Christians in a local church. It is intended for fellow Christians in a similar situation, in the belief that these same issues are being made alive for many. It is an attempt to give perspective, not to find final answers.

I

'Restoration'—First Principles

The three 'R's

There are a number of words in use in the church which indicate a perspective on its life and which signal loyalty to a movement within it. By some accident of history and of vocabulary most of them seem to begin with 'R'. By some process of necessity most of them also seem to provide a handy title for one or other journal advocating a certain line.

Reformation

We are all acquainted with this movement. Here we are on solid ground. The Reformation is long enough ago to have become respectable. Even Catholics now write books about Luther. Some even agree with him. The Reformation era is a fascinating and, in many respects, a noble episode in human history. The face of the church was transformed by it; the issues at stake within it are immense. How is a man justified before God? By faith, alone! To what is man's salvation to be attributed? To grace, alone! Where does authority lie in the church? With Scripture, alone!

Daily we live in the good of what was achieved at the Reformation. To be acquainted with and committed to the

Reformation issues can bring only good, provided we also understand what the Reformers themselves tried to say, that reformation is an ongoing process, that the church is always being reformed, that is, changed for the better, under the word of God.

Counterbalancing this, we must acknowledge that Christians, even Protestant Christians, have a tendency (which they share with the rest of the human race) to canonize their heroes or their heroic epochs. Like the children of Israel they are able to take an instrument of past blessing, such as the bronze snake in the wilderness used by God in healing them in Numbers 21:4–9, and make it an object of idolatrous worship in a later generation rivalling God and requiring dethroning (see 2 Kings 18:4). When we idolize movements of God in the past we should be careful that we do not miss the point in the present. What God requires is not people who will protest a loyal and fervent attachment to past worthies in order to bask in the reflected glory, but people who will be radically obedient now to what was made plain through those servants.

Renewal

Then we have *renewal.* By the 1960s the Pentecostal experience of the early years of the century began to permeate the historic denominations. This had, of course, happened in isolated ways before but usually led to 'schism' as the 'renewed' factions in a church either left or were ejected to form new Pentecostal assemblies. The difference in the 'charismatic renewal' was that people were renewed and for the most part remained as loyal members of their churches, committed to renewal from within.

The choice of the word 'renewal' to describe this process is an apt one. As well as reflecting the newness of a charismatic experience it also implies no radical disjunction between what was and what came to be. Those who were being renewed were simply experiencing in a fresh way what had been latent in the faith they received all along and was now coming to life with fresh vigour. Renewed people sought to see themselves not as different in kind from any others in their church, simply different in the degree and extent of their experience.

Involvement in renewal has been exciting. Old barriers have been broken down as believers have come together not so much on the basis of a doctrinal agreement as of an experiential reality. The presence and power of God have become evident in many churches of quite different churchmanship making for growth and life. In place of the old vertical denominational divisions the churches are now more accurately divided horizontally between those who are in renewal and those who are not. Renewed Baptists will more easily join a renewed Anglican church than an unrenewed Baptist church. The face of the church has radically altered under the influence of renewal and is set to do so more as the renewal movement, far from being on the wane as some suggest, gathers momentum and maturity and works out both its impact and its implications.

It is here that we get near to the point of this book. Charismatic renewal is a movement which makes for radical obedience. It takes us back to Jesus. Jesus is exalted as Lord, the Scriptures sparkle with a new vitality, the Holy Spirit warms the heart of the believer making for sacrificial and costly service. The honest believer who reads his revitalized Scriptures must come to terms with the fact that the church, institutionalized and corrupted as she is, is not what she should be, not what God wills her to be and not what Scripture makes plain she can be. As he reads he comes to certain conclusions about the nature of the church God desires. The impetus towards renewal thus becomes an impetus towards reformation and faithfulness in the corporate structures of the church. The renewed individual aspires to live out his life within a renewed church.

This is where his problems begin. He begins to challenge the status quo and the status quo responds more often than not with resistance. Sometimes the resistance is overcome, sometimes not, but it is at this point that the view of the church he embraces determines his course of action. Those who lean towards a view of the church as an established/state/national/hierarchical institution will seek renewal within that structure; those who incline towards a free-church ecclesiology or doctrine of the church will be less patient with this view. Since we will look at this tension elsewhere we will leave it for the time being, except to say that it is precisely at this point that the charismatic renewal movement is tending to divide today, so that the actual issue at stake is the view of the church we embrace and the consequent policy of action we follow. This is also why baptism is, and will continue to be, a particular focus of tension, since our attitudes to baptism grow out of our particular understanding of the church.

The heart of the renewed experience today is where it has always been whenever the church has experienced renewal in the past, that is in the encounter with Christ through the Scriptures in the power and vitality of the Holy Spirit.

Contrary to popular opinion the difference between Martin Luther and his Catholic opponents was not that he knew the Bible and they did not. The writings of his opponents are full of references to Scripture. The crucial difference was that to Luther the Bible had become a place where he encountered Christ and knew that he had been justified by faith in him. No longer was it a textbook to be quoted along with other textbooks to prove a point. It was a means of grace, a place where he dealt with Christ and Christ dealt with him through his word.

To grasp this is essential. Evangelical Christians have been so taken up with the debate about Scripture, its inerrancy or otherwise, the nature of its inspiration, its historical reliability, etc., that they are in danger of missing the point. It is the function of Scripture, not its form, which is of crucial importance. This is where Paul lays the emphasis in 2 Timothy 3:16 where he asserts its inspiration and goes on to assert that it 'is *useful* for teaching, rebuking, correcting and training in righteousness'. For Paul the consequence of Scripture's inspiration is not to deduce a set of theories about its form but to assert its function in our encounter with God. Renewal begins with Scripture as the place where the words point us to the Word of God in whom are life, wisdom and knowledge and whom to know is freedom. This was, is and must always be the essence of renewal; this is where the Holy Spirit takes us again and again—to Christ as Scripture bears witness to him.

We have already used the word 'radical' on a number of occasions. To be radical means to go to the roots of an issue. The radical view of the church as advocated in this book grows out of a simple principle. The radical believer is so because he is prepared to look at his faith and his church in the light of their roots. He is prepared to go back to the Scriptures and allow them to shed the decisive light on how things should be. He is prepared to be informed, excited and challenged not by the way things are but by the way things should be as witnessed to by the New Testament. He insists that God has revealed his will in Christ and in Scripture's testimony to him and is prepared to allow this to be what shapes his attitudes, actions and aspirations however much at variance this may seem to be with the established order of things. This principle does not contradict the principles affirmed by the need for 'reformation' and 'renewal'. It is to be seen as being in harmony with them and, indeed, as growing out of them. Furthermore, it gives rise to all that is intended by this book's use of 'restoration', which it confidently advocates. Renewal must lead to both reformation and restoration.

The reclaiming and re-experiencing of Jesus as Lord through the Holy Spirit cannot be allowed to dissipate because of our refusal to pursue the process to its conclusion. Luther grasped that the church needed to be reformed, that abuses needed to be rectified. We still face the challenge of bringing the corporate life of the church into conformity with God's will. The hardening and destructive effect in the church of mere tradition, vested interest and unbiblical practices hinders God's work. The church therefore requires a continual process of *reformation*.

Restoration

But reformation of what is, needs to be accompanied by a *restoration* of what is not. Looked at in the light of the New Testament there are dimensions of experience, behaviour, ministry, life and expectation which are wholly or partially missing from the church as it is today. These things need to be restored and we should not rest until they are. This is what is meant here by the word 'restoration', and this ideal or principle is not a new one. As we shall see, it is deeply rooted in the life of the church and has been so for many centuries. In fact the principle of restoration is simply an extension of the Reformation principle of 'Scripture alone' whereby Scripture is our rule for faith and conduct.

For Luther, the crucial issue of how to be right with God came into focus when he discovered the Pauline teaching of justification by faith. Once he had discovered this he was then put in the dilemma of having to relate this to the received teaching of the Roman Catholic Church which asserted that salvation was not by faith alone but required the ongoing mediation of the church to sustain faith and holiness. Who was right? Where did authority lie? He answered this by exalting the authority of Scripture over the authority of the church. The church stood under the authority of the word of God and was to be tested against it. Once this principle was accepted it could not be long before this same principle of the authority of the Bible was applied not just to the issue of justification but to the whole of the church's life.

How did what was received match up against the Scriptures? The effects of applying this question were dramatic not only for the church but for the whole of the social order since fidelity to Scripture would require wholesale and far-reaching change in both church and state. It argues for the thoroughgoing application of the authority of God's word at all levels and not just at the level of personal faith.

Traditionally, evangelicals have opposed liberal theology for its reduction of the authority of Scripture. They have argued for the primacy, the inerrancy and the infallibility of Holy Scripture. They have held a high view of Scripture and regarded this as the shibboleth of soundness. Those who did not toe this line were to be regarded as virtual renegades. Yet it is curiously possible to combine a high theoretical view of Scripture with a practical denial of its authority for us.

Illustrative of this point are the brilliant systems of dispensational theology which have effectively robbed us of the word by denying the normative nature of the New Testament for the church today. 'Dispensationalist' refers to a theological posture whereby the biblical revelation is divided into distinct ages in which God adopted different methods of working for different people. In most of these systems the apostolic age (that which is covered in the New Testament) is therefore seen as an exceptional period. We are not to expect the church to be like that now. It is not normative for us. Of course it is our duty to believe and defend the fact that all these things once happened precisely as is described but there is no need to believe or hope that the same might or should happen today. Not all Christian thinkers who adopt this position would be happy to have themselves described as dispensationalists. Some would specifically be on record as opposing dispensational systems; but they can accurately be described, whether they like it or not, as neo-dispensationalist since the normative authority of the New Testament is in practice denied.

'Restoration' turns this theology on its head. Far from arguing that what we are or experience in the church today is normative while the New Testament is exceptional, it assumes that the New Testament revelation is the norm for the church, and that we are falling short of it. Our task is not to justify or rationalize or even theologize our present state of decline but to seek a restoration of the New Testament norm. Our present state may be the average, but it is not

God's norm. It may be that when we compare ourselves with each other we do not look too bad, but when we examine ourselves in the light of Scripture our churches and church practices are found to be profoundly inadequate.

This is the only way we can take the authority of the Bible seriously. It is a curious theology that argues for the authority of Scripture and then denies its relevance; it is an equally curious theology that asserts the authority of Scripture in relation to personal salvation and doctrine but denies it in relation to the nature and form of the church.

It is time to unmuzzle the Bible, to free it from our theological grids which have caused us to ignore large parts of it or to filter them out so that we do not hear them and are not disturbed by them. It is time to stop defending its authority in theory and start submitting to it in practice. If we are to live under the word of God we should do so wholeheartedly and thoroughly and should seek to see the church restored in the fullness of its life.

Others object by fudging the issue. Since the New Testament is not one monolithic whole, how can it provide the norm for the church today? It would be easy to accept the New Testament as normative, it is claimed, if the New Testament seemed to have a norm, but as it is what we find there is a rich diversity of theologies, since different writers present different pictures of Christ, different churches seem to operate with different church orders and generally the whole scene is one of fluidity and even formlessness.

It is true that the New Testament presents us with such diversity but the diversity which it portrays also has an underlying unity. The theological models used by its writers are coherent and complementary. For instance, different strands of the New Testament use different words and concepts to speak of who Christ is. They employ overlapping images of the fullness of Christ and do not leave us at the end of the day with several Christs but one. Equally, there are traces of different orders of church life demonstrating the pragmatic organizational skills of the church leaders according to the situation. But it is not difficult to recognize the factors which were common to them all and which made them recognizable to each other beyond the confines of culture and locality. The diversity in Scripture is a warning against rigidity in interpretation. It does not make the search for scriptural principles which can be applied in a variety of situations impossible. Nor does it negate the underlying unity of the various strands of New Testament theology.

It is a mistake to see the principle of restoration as a rigid and slavish attempt to decode the New Testament and to bring life into a sterile conformity with it. Granted, some restorationists have adopted this attitude and treated the Scriptures like the blueprint for the tabernacle given to Moses on the mountain, but this is not actually the point. Rather the point is that the New Testament is our place of orientation. It is where we start from and return to. It is where we stand to hear the voice and to understand the will of the living God, and from where we survey the land that lies before us.

To treat Scripture as a computer codebook is to mistreat Scripture. We meet *God* as we confront and wrestle with Scripture (and if need be argue with it); it is in this process that the knowledge of God is disclosed to us. But it is to the light of Scripture that we must bring our traditions, our prejudices, our practices and our expectations in order to see them as they truly are. This is a very costly business. What the New Testament presents us with in relation to the church is not a static model which it is our duty to implement in all circumstances but a living *theology* of the church which it is our task first of all to understand and then to give expression to in our age and culture in the power of the Holy Spirit. This theology of the church is coherent but allows for great variety and flexibility in its application.

A further point is worth making: it is false logic to assume on the basis of diversity in Scripture that all forms of diversity are acceptable today. Yet this is the deduction which some would want to make. Because there are interlocking interpretations of the person of Christ in Scripture it does not mean that any interpretation of him will do. Similarly, because the New Testament pictures different ways of ordering the life of the church, we are not to assume that God is careless about how it is done today. Not at all. Instead we are to take great care that the church of today rings true with the church of the apostles. Surely this is a far from unreasonable task to attempt.

The thesis of this chapter, then, is that in order to take the authority of Scripture seriously, in order to live under the word and to hear what God has to say through it on the whole range of issues which concern him, we should understand that the new covenant revelation, the revelation of God in Christ as witnessed to by the apostles, is to be seen as God's norm for the church. This should not lead to a slavish attempt to reproduce in our own strength what we cannot in fact do: it should lead us to seek God for the renewal and restoration of his kingdom among us so that what he wills takes place. This is a commitment to a process of recovery and discovery and it is open-ended. We cannot claim that in any given example we have the fullness of this recovery since there is always more that we may not yet be seeing. But we can commit ourselves to the process.

Restoration language

Having, for the sake of clarity, expressed this basic principle of restoration first, it is necessary to say some more about restoration language. First of all we will look at the various dimensions of the concept of restoration language in theology and then more specifically at models of restoration drawn from Scripture which are influential in the contemporary church.

Firstly, there is *the language of personal restoration*. The primary focus in Scripture is upon the work of God in restoring lost humanity to himself. The biblical analysis of man is of a creature who is alienated from God, from himself, from his neighbour and from creation. He is fragmented and broken, caught in an internal and external discord and yet able to discover salvation and restoration through Christ who has come to be the head of a new humanity, a last Adam giving life to a new race of people being remade in the image of the Liberator and Redeemer.

Thus the language of personal restoration merges into *the language of corporate restoration*. Not only do we discover healing for our inward being through the forgiveness of sins and its actualization within us, we discover a 'healing in community'. Not only our inner selves but also our relationships are capable of being redeemed. The church is the expression of this in God's intention. It is a demonstration of the new race which is coming into being. It is marked by love and unselfish service. It is also marked by a weakness which points beyond itself to one who dwells with his people and who is the source of their life. Most of all, this 'community in process of being restored' is a sign of a coming age.

The language of corporate restoration therefore merges into *the language of cosmic restoration*. For God's intention is to restore everything that has been alienated; it is to heal all that has been wounded. The church is a sign of what God wills to do in the whole creation in the fullness of time—to restore it to himself and to his eternal purpose. The prophets speak of the restoration of all things and of a new heaven and a new earth. Paul speaks of the creation groaning in labour pains as it awaits its deliverance and fulfilment; he speaks of all things being summed up in Christ, through whom ultimately all things will be restored. This is a glorious vision and it indicates the role of the church in this process—it is to be a reconciled, restored presence in the world *now*, pointing to and preparing for a complete restoration which is yet to come. We are both the sign and the agent of this process. How important it is, then, for the church to be free to be the church. How inextricably linked are God's working in his church and the destiny of the whole creation.

These are magnificent themes and deserve much attention. The word 'restoration' is being used here in a different way from the more limited definition already given in this chapter. For the sake of clarity it is helpful to distinguish this although it must also be said that the broader canvas highlights the importance of there being a restored church which is an adequate witness to and a sign of God's saving activity.

Models of restoration

Once persuaded about the need for restoration it is natural to begin searching Scripture for models which will help us put flesh on the bones of this concept. Since the New Testament church was not in need of restoration in the sense already outlined, it being itself an example of how the church could be (despite the shortcomings which Scripture does not seek to disguise), there is a twofold tendency to look to the Old Testament for models of how to enter into restoration and to employ these in preaching and teaching for the edification of the church.

In contemporary restoration teaching, several such Old Testament motifs and models recur. We shall examine these shortly. Before doing so we must be aware of a danger not always fully recognized (by preachers or people alike) in restoration circles: the Old Testament, of itself, is not to be normative for us. This is an important point which goes to the heart of the restoration principle itself. Jesus and the New Testament are normative for us, so no part of the Old Testament can be treated a-Christologically and accorded this status. The restoration principle takes us back to Christ, not beyond Christ. Any teaching which finds its norm anywhere other than in Christ himself is actually a violation of the principle of restoration and is to be resisted.

This does not mean that the Old Testament is of no value; far from it. It does mean, however, that Old Testament material is illustrative rather than normative and that it must always be interpreted through Christ, who is the fulfilment of the law, and not apart from him. No part of the Old Testament can be abstracted and exalted as the determining model/picture for the church or serve as the key to action for our present situation. If it is taken in this way it is bound to lead us away from Christ and therefore into some form of bondage. Take these three examples.

The promised land

The children of Israel were rescued out of the bondage and slavery of Egypt. Under the able and God-appointed leadership of Moses they were lead into the wilderness and because of the disobedience of the majority were destined to wander there for forty years. In this time they were transformed from being a disorderly rabble into an ordered army ready to enter the promised land where they would live in a settled community under God's rule. They were at a transitional stage, on the move and pursuing a vision that was inspired in them by God. As such their experiences are instructive for those of us in the present day who are in a period of transition, pursuing a vision similarly inspired by God.

We are able to learn much from their desert life and apply it by way of illustration to our own experiences. We can identify with the pain Moses felt in leading the people, with the fear and confusion and the moaning of the people. We can draw comfort from the way God intervened and protected his people, and we have every right to do so because, according to 1 Corinthians 10:6, 'These things occurred as examples, to keep us from setting our hearts on evil things as they did.' They are warnings to us and it is right to interpret them Christologically as does Paul in verses 1–4 of that chapter, seeing that the One who sustained them in the wilderness was Christ himself. To use Scripture in this way to shed light on our present situation is totally in line with Paul's words in 2 Timothy 3:16 that all Scripture is useful for teaching and correction. However to push it further than this is not legitimate.

It is possible, though not advisable, to extend the significance of these verses by building on the word 'examples' which literally means 'types' and say that these verses are actually a type of the restoration of the church and are recorded for the benefit of us who live in the age of prophetic fulfilment. Taken this way, the promised land is a type of the renewed, restored church into which we are called to move, and the other features of the exodus and wilderness narrative becoming controlling, normative directions as to how we are to make the transition. Thus Moses and later Joshua represent the church leaders called by God, whom we are to obey; the unwillingness of the people represents that proportion of the Christian population who are unwilling to make the transition; the river Jordan becomes the crucial entry point into the new territory of God's government.

What is wrong with this approach is that in moving from illustration to norm we are actually making our standard something other than Jesus himself, and we are at the same time violating the text of Scripture, since in 1 Corinthians 10 Paul is not instructing people about restoration but about overconfidence and arrogance.

The Davidic kingdom

A similar trend can be discerned when the Davidic kingdom is taken as a model for the restored church. In Acts 15:16–18 James quotes the prophecy of Amos that David's fallen tent will be restored. Building on this verse, some restoration teachers have constructed a theology of restoration around the concept of an end-time restoration of a Davidic kingdom manifesting the same characteristics as the Davidic reign, such as the government of God expressed through delegated authorities, celebration, worship, proclamation and creativity. In his book *Built to Last*, Ron Trudinger develops this line and argues for the restoration of the Davidic kingdom. It is significant that in the chapter which deals with David's tabernacle, there are many references to David, but not one to Jesus.

The point is this. We may draw many illustrative lessons

from David's reign, and indeed we should do so, but only when we have understood David via Jesus. If we make the reign of David normative for church life today (as appears to be happening in some circles) we risk being led away from Christ and at key points will find ourselves moving off-centre.

In Trudinger's book, much is made of the concept of delegated authority, and this is rooted in the kingdom of David. Yet we look in vain for this concept or a case for it being made in this way in the teaching of Jesus or of the early church. If we make David the norm and fit Jesus in afterwards we will be led astray. David is a type of Christ but there are elements of his kingdom which are clearly inconsistent with Jesus—David was a man of war, Jesus was not; David had earthly power, Jesus refused it; David built a hierarchical system of government, Jesus spoke against hierarchies. David can never be the norm for the church—Jesus must be. Our interpretation of David must be seen through Jesus, his greater Son who eclipsed him.

Exile and restoration

A third model for restoration is found in the exile of Judah in Babylon and her subsequent restoration to Zion. It is interesting that songs drawn from the restoration age of Judah figure prominently in current restoration circles, speaking as they do of the return from captivity of the people of God. In this approach to restoration, Babylon denotes the compromised, institutional church out of which the people of God are to depart to be restored to Zion, the true city of God, in order to commence the work of rebuilding the temple and the city. Nehemiah comes into his own at this point and his methods for rebuilding Jerusalem are seen to be 'apostolic' in their significance; that is, concerned with the rebuilding of the church along proper lines.

Again, there is no objection to using these sections of the word of God as illustrations of situations in which we might find ourselves today. To preach from them in this vein is fully acceptable and in the best tradition. To suggest, however, that the restoration of the church in our day and age is precisely that to which they refer, although as types of the coming reality, is yet again to find a scriptural norm where we have no right to find one and is to take us where we do not wish to go, that is, away from Christ. The ultimate end of such approaches is—while appearing scriptural and sounding spiritual—to take us into forms of church life which have little or nothing to do with Jesus because they have not been derived from him. What we end up with may indeed be 'scriptural' but scriptural in a way wrongly understood because Scripture should not be interpreted apart from the Christ to whom it bears witness.

The principle of restoration, when properly applied, is one which always takes us back to Jesus and the immediate witness to him in the apostolic church. Models of restoration which divert us from this end ultimately frustrate the work of restoration since Christ is all.

The fourth 'R'

As with the other positions outlined in this chapter, *revival* also has its advocates. To hear some voices, all the church needs is revival and nothing else really matters. Some carry this position to an extreme which allows them to do absolutely nothing while they wait for revival to come. Of course, while they do this they show themselves to be foreign to those in the past who have actually been instrumental in revival's coming. For revival has never 'just come'; it has been prayed for, longed for and prepared for, and it has certainly not come without prior cost to one or other section of God's people.

It would be foolish to divorce the need for revival from the need for reformation, renewal and restoration. Revival has been at its most potent when 1.) it has had at its heart a serious and penetrating preaching of the word of God which is characteristic of the reformation process; 2.) it has had as its precursor a renewing movement in the hearts at least of some of God's people who have been warmed towards him and have sought him fervently; 3.) it has required the context of biblically-based practices and expectations in order to be properly conserved and advanced. The fact must be that, although God can and does work sovereignly whenever and wherever he chooses to do so, he seems to seek out people whose hearts are after his own heart, and wherever he finds them he acts. There is something about God which seeks to co-operate with men rather than to work without regard to them.

Nobody can claim that if a church has a heart for restoration and is pursuing that path then revival will automatically follow. Were we to assume that, God would no doubt do precisely the opposite to show himself free and to confound our foolish wisdom. We are, however, entitled to believe that where the power of God is visited upon those who are genuinely seeking to be as faithful to revelation as they possibly can be, then the results will bring more glory to God than would otherwise be the case. Surely our concern should be to do the work God has given us to do in the way in which it is best done, and who best knows this but God himself, who has spoken in his word?

The history of revivals is an exciting study. There is nothing quite so thrilling as seeing the visitation of God upon his church and a community. Perhaps we would be more acquainted with such visitations if we learned how not to grieve the Holy Spirit by our disobedience. After all, the Holy Spirit is given to those who obey God.

Reformation, renewal, restoration and revival are therefore not options that we may choose between but dimensions of what we should always be seeking after.

In this chapter we have set out the main elements of restoration. We have sought to define it as a working principle which takes the authority of Scripture seriously and which sees God's revelation of himself in Christ as the norm around which all other things should be built. It is a principle born of the desire to live under the word of God. It is not a mechanical, rigid method of re-creating the unrepeatable conditions of the first century; it is a commitment to orientating ourselves, in the church of God, towards and by the New Testament revelation.

In the following chapters we shall attempt to apply the principle to the specifics of Christian experience, church structure, doctrine and behaviour. We shall also attempt to show that the vision of the restored church is not a recent phenomenon but is deeply rooted in Christian history.

2

Restoration in History

For centuries, the word 'Anabaptist' served as a byword for fanaticism and revolution as a result of a disastrous episode in the German town of Münster during the years 1534–35. In the ferment which accompanied the Reformation a whole range of social and political grievances began to surface in Europe, finding expression in religious experience and language.

The so-called Peasants' Revolt, or Peasant War, broke out in the Black Forest in 1524 and spread rapidly, involving in time some 300,000 armed peasants. Their programme was a twelve-point demand for far-reaching reforms in the church and the social order. Their leader was a preacher called Thomas Müntzer who called for a new age to be brought in and organized his followers into armed bands to assist it on its way. He approved of direct and violent action to establish the true gospel. Originally a supporter of Luther, he turned against him because of what he perceived to be his compromise. Luther in his turn vehemently opposed Müntzer and his cause and called for the sword to be used against the peasants. Müntzer was defeated in battle at Frankenhausen in May 1525 and subsequently executed. The whole episode damaged the cause of the Reformation greatly by alienating the established church from the peasantry and asserting its dependence on the military power of the state.

The Münster episode was only to extend this damage. Under the influence of an Anabaptist pioneer, Melchior Hofmann, the Anabaptist cause began to develop after 1531 in Münster and was symbolized by the practice of believers' baptism, but under the more sinister influence of Jan Matthys and Jan van Leiden the cause began to depart from the peaceful views of Hofmann and to pursue a policy of violence against the ungodly. In February 1534, in the cause of the restitution of the apostolic church, the city hall was seized and all who refused baptism were expelled from the city. Münster then became the 'New Jerusalem' attracting to itself the desperate and the persecuted, already rendered extreme by the hostility of the authorities.

Bishop Franz, the local ruler, laid siege to the city, giving impetus to the view already developing within Münster that the 'children of Jacob' were to help God to annihilate the 'children of Esau'! Imagining that he could disperse the besieging army outside the city walls, Matthys was slain and was succeeded by Jan van Leiden who—in addition to promoting armed resistance—instituted community of goods and polygamy, the former finding its inspiration in the Jerusalem church, the latter in the Old Testament. Eventually van Leiden was to be proclaimed 'King of the New Zion' and was to erect his throne in the market square. The final act in the drama came in June 1535 when, with help from within, the city fell to the bishop's forces. Van Leiden and the other leaders were cruelly tortured, displayed around the country, and executed in January 1536. Their corpses were hung in cages from the church tower, where the cages still hang. Most of the male population was also executed.

For centuries Münster has dominated the popular and scholarly estimation of anabaptism. It has suited the purposes of anti-Anabaptist propaganda to make much of the incident and in this way the true nature of anabaptism has been obscured. The purpose of this chapter is to expose the issues that gave rise to the development of sixteenth-century anabaptism, of which Münster anabaptism is not only unrepresentative but a gross distortion. Far from reflecting mainstream anabaptism, the specific features of Münster (as for instance the linking of church and state, the use of violence and the prominence given to the Old Testament) are more characteristic of the official churches against which the Anabaptists were in reaction.

Who were the Anabaptists and what did they stand for? This question is more easily asked than answered for the simple reason that the word 'anabaptist' is used to describe not one coherent movement but a whole collection of disparate radical groups, many of whom had little in common. Some groups were 'spiritualists', which, in distinction from the modern use of the term, means that they exalted the immediate guidance of the Holy Spirit above the authority of Scripture. Others were clearly heretics of a unitarian and antitrinitarian kind.

Fortunately, the immense volume of research carried out in this century enables us to lay aside the sweeping generalizations based upon anti-Anabaptist polemic and to define the various radical groups more accurately. Franklin H. Littell has attempted the following working definition—*the Anabaptists proper were those in the radical Reformation who gathered and disciplined a 'true Church' . . . upon the apostolic pattern as they understood it.* (The Origins of Sectarian Protestantism, page xvii.) Working with this definition, the origins of anabaptism are to be traced to the group commonly known as the evangelical Anabaptists of Zurich.

Zurich was one of the three main centres of the Reformation in Europe. As Luther was discovering the nature of grace and faith in Wittenberg, parallel developments were taking place in the life of Ulrich Zwingli, people's priest at the Great Minster in Zurich. Having encountered the Bible in its original languages, Zwingli began to reform Zurich, working carefully with the city council.

Zwingli was himself more radical than Luther and less of a

traditionalist. The reformation movement in Switzerland gained impetus from house meetings and reading groups in which lay people learnt how to interpret and discuss the Bible. It was out of these groups that the leaders of the Anabaptist movement emerged. Men such as Conrad Grebel, Felix Manz and Georg Blaurock were themselves well educated and from prominent families or backgrounds. Initially they had shared enthusiastically with Zwingli in his rediscovery of the Bible and its theology, but in due course they began to dispute with him because their study of the Bible was leading them further away from the status quo than he was prepared to go.

Like Luther (and later Calvin), Zwingli had committed himself to a gradualist approach to reformation. Desiring to carry the whole town with him and recognizing that he required the support of the town council to do this, his policy was to preach the word and allow the word to do its work of persuading. Of necessity this meant that even while preaching against certain practices in the church (e.g. the mass) those practices remained until the town council decided to abolish or reform them. Zwingli himself continued to celebrate the mass in which he did not believe.

In his early period Zwingli, again like Luther, espoused some very radical ideas. At first he opposed infant baptism, finding it absent from the New Testament; but, as to abolish infant baptism and practise believers' baptism would have struck a blow at the church, the state and the connection between the two (membership of church and state being synonymous), he retreated and held to the official state church position. In the eyes of his more radical associates Zwingli was living in compromise. To allow the state to dictate the degree or the pace of one's obedience to God's word was in their eyes to exalt the state above God.

By October 1523 the radicals were committed to a different approach. Rejecting the policy of a slow (and possibly only partial) reformation of the official church, they became committed to a policy of restitution or restoration of apostolic Christianity on a thoroughgoing basis. As Zwingli argued for infant baptism, they now argued in public disputations for the baptism of believers. On January 21st 1525, under threat of expulsion because of their views and in a late-night meeting at the home of Felix Manz, the following incident took place:

> After prayer Georg Cajacob (Blaurock) stood up and begged Conrad Grebel for God's sake to baptise him with true Christian baptism upon his faith and confession. And because he was kneeling with such a request and desire Conrad baptised him, because there was no minister ordained for such an action. When that had happened the others in the same way desired of Georg that he baptise them, which he did at their request. Thus in the great fear of God they committed one another to the name of the Lord and installing one another in the ministry of the Gospel, began to teach and to keep the faith. Thereby began separation from the world and from its evil works. (Quoted in Cornelius J. Dyck (ed.), *An Introduction to Mennonite History*, p. 34.)

With this action the radicals moved from merely opposing infant baptism to a positive commitment to the baptism of believers. In so doing, it should be understood, they were breaking an ancient law, promulgated in the fourth century against the Donatist schism in the church. The Donatists had broken from the Catholic Church in the belief that it was a compromised church. They re-baptized Catholics, and a law was subsequently passed forbidding this. Now 're-baptism' was punishable by death. In the eyes of the state church the radicals were re-baptizing, hence the name 'anabaptist' which means a 're-baptizer' and which when applied to the radicals became simultaneously an accusation.

In their own eyes, of course, the radicals were administering true baptism for the first time. They simply called themselves 'brethren'. Having baptized, the brethren had put themselves outside the law. From now on they were to feel the full force of it. For the radicals baptism was also an ordination. As different ones of them began to scatter from Zurich they went out as missionaries and within a short time radical groups were established in a number of centres, the first coming into being in early February 1525 in the village of Zollikon just near Zurich through the influence of Georg Blaurock. This church, which in a short time was worn down through persecution, has the claim to be the first free church of the modern era.

For most of those baptized, arrest and exile followed swiftly. Zwingli was as vehemently opposed to these 'schismatics' as they now felt towards him. In the eyes of the radicals, those who refused to go the whole way of obedience were now out to persecute those who did not and whose only desire was to be faithful to what they had learnt from the Bible to which Zwingli had directed them. The story of the ensuing years is one of amazing growth and remarkable suffering. Anabaptism spread rapidly as the brethren went from house to house and village to village. The Zurich leaders had only a short time to make their mark. Conrad Grebel, now a fugitive, became a victim of the plague in August 1526. Felix Manz was among the first Anabaptist martyrs. Sentenced to death by drowning (the third baptism!) he was drowned in the waters of the Limmat with his arms and legs tied securely together on January 5th 1527. His final words were, 'Into your hands, O Lord, I commend my spirit.' Georg Blaurock was severely beaten on the same day but continued to exercise a fiery and effective ministry until he was burnt at the stake in 1529. After 1529, the number of martyrs increased rapidly. In both Protestant and Catholic lands the Anabaptists were harried, persecuted and in some places successfully eradicated. The eventual toll of martyrs has been placed in excess of 4,000. Many of them displayed remarkable steadfastness and courage in the face of death.

It is important to stress that the real issue between Zwingli and the radical brethren was not baptism but the nature of the church. Zwingli was out to reform the church but (as Luther had already conceded and as Calvin was to do) he accepted without question the concept of the sacral state which he had inherited and which had prevailed since the Edict of Milan in A.D. 311, when Christianity was officially tolerated, eventually to become the official religion of the Empire. According to this view, church and state were identified and linked. Membership of the church and of the state were identical. The state legislated in all matters of religion and compelled conformity by the power of the sword and of the magistrate. The Reformers continued in this respect the policy and practice of Rome and because of their reliance upon the magistrate are referred to as 'the magisterial Reformers'. In their turn the Reformers used the power of the state against Catholics, Anabaptists and heretics. The Reformation was enforced by the power of the princes.

As the radicals studied their Bibles, they went beyond Zwingli in their understanding of the church and began to see the anomaly of allowing the secular state to dictate to the church the terms in which it should or should not obey Christ. The conflict between what Scripture taught and what the state allowed led them to a reappraisal of what the church was and was not. By 1540 a consensus of belief broadly characterized the Anabaptist movement which we may attempt to describe as follows:

The believers' church

The radical brethren asserted above all else that the church was composed of those and only those who had experienced the regenerating work of the Holy Spirit. In affirming this they dissented from the concept that had prevailed for centuries that membership of church and state were coextensive. The state church concept operated with the notion that all who were resident in a locality were automatically members of the church. Infant baptism was the sign and instrument of this inclusion. Salvation depended upon belonging to the church thus constituted; and the institutional resources of the church—its priesthood, sacraments and mediation—were the channels of grace for here and hereafter.

Against Rome, the radicals asserted that this was false. The true church was not an institution or a hierarchy but a brotherhood, a family composed of those who had faith. Although Luther recovered the element of justification by faith, the Anabaptists stressed not just the forensic element of being justified but the inner transformation and renewal of the individual which led to discipleship and the imitation of Christ.

Believers' baptism developed from the concept of the believers' church. Since infants could neither repent nor freely believe they should not be baptized. The evidence of the early church was that faith was voluntarily entered into and that the baptism of the believer was accompanied by a thorough transformation of life.

Discipleship was not an option for the Christian, but an essential. He was required to walk with Christ even if this walk led to the baptism of suffering. The disciple was to be a nonconformist who cheerfully accepted persecution for Jesus' sake.

For most Anabaptists this nonconformity implied a refusal to swear oaths (in obedience to Jesus' words) and a non-involvement in state functions (such as serving as magistrates) since church and state were to be kept separate. Magistrates should not involve themselves in matters of faith—to exceed this was to go beyond their sphere. Since magistrates were in fact being required to do this within a sacral state, the disciple ought not to function in this capacity.

The Anabaptists pioneered what has come to be called the 'free church' concept or the 'congregational' view of the church. The local church did not depend for its validity on its relationship to bishop, pope, hierarchy or state, but on the presence of Christ in the midst. In this way each congregation could participate in decision-making and in the disciplining of its members.

From the first, among Anabaptists, discipline was understood to be one of the characteristic functions of the church, and baptism, as well as the expression of personal faith, was the acceptance by the individual of the authority of the congregation to discipline. The power of the believers' church resided not in its ability to wield the sword and use secular power to coerce, but in its power to exclude the immoral and wayward from its fellowship.

Pioneers though they were of the recovery of biblical truth, the magisterial Reformers stopped short of implementing a fully biblical theology of the church. This is not to say that they did not perceive it. One of the best descriptions of the believers' church concept comes from the pen of Luther in his early years. In his pursuit of a 'truly evangelical order' he envisaged that the believers would

> sign their names and meet alone in a house somewhere to pray, to read, to baptize, to receive the sacrament, and do other Christian works. According to this order, those who do not lead Christian lives could be known, reproved, corrected, cast out or excommunicated, according to the rule of Christ (Mt 18:15–17). Here one could also solicit benevolent gifts to be willingly given and distributed to the poor, according to St Paul's example (2 Cor 9). Here would be no need of much and elaborate singing. Here one could set out a brief and neat order for baptism and the sacrament and centre everything on the word, prayer and love. (Quoted in Donald F. Durnbaugh, *The Believers' Church,* page 3.)

These gatherings for worship, Luther envisaged, would not be for the mixed assembly of believer and unbeliever but for those 'who want to be Christians in earnest and who profess the gospel with hand and mouth'. The Anabaptists would have agreed with every word! A better description of the radical vision of the church could hardly be found and yet, in the event, both Luther and Zwingli held back from implementing the vision and stayed with the inherited notion of a state church linked with and dependent upon the secular power. If the Anabaptists committed a crime it was that of being more consistent than their mentors.

Fall and restoration

A further crucial insight of the radical brethren relates to their understanding that the church had in its history undergone a 'fall' from the original grace in which it stood and the task now was to see it 'restored' to its original purity. Their intention was to restore something old, not invent something new. The sources of this insight were in the study of Scripture and in their actual experience of the fallen church.

The title which has been given to this approach is 'primitivism', a word describing those whose guiding vision is the vision of the early church. For the Anabaptists this meant that they were able to pass judgement on the contemporary church via the criterion of the early church. Their dream of the early church was accompanied by an eschatological vision which hoped for an age of restoration in the future.

In these twin visions lies the motivating power of the radical movement. The concept of the fall of the church is the counterpart of the biblical doctrine of the fall of man. Man fell and now the church has fallen. The early years of the church's history revealed a church which was faithful and pure and because of this it was also a persecuted church where to be a Christian was a disadvantage and therefore a costly commitment. The fall of the church was dated from the time of Constantine when the church, released from the pressure of persecution and elevated to a position of power, ceased to be the community of brothers in inspired congregations under charismatic leadership it had been and became progressively institutionalized, compromised and paganized. The fall of the church lasted until the time of the Anabaptists themselves and included the Reformers who, although they began the revival of true religion, failed to carry it through to the decisive point of restoration. This task began with the Anabaptists themselves who began to rescue the church from its illegitimate and unbiblical involvement with the state and its power.

Under the Roman Empire religion had played a significant

part in binding the empire together. For the emperors, religion was an agent of political rule providing cohesion and unity, where religious dissent (with the exception of the Jews, who for a time were treated as an exception and cultivated because of their economic value) was rigorously quashed. The state religion was very accommodating and would incorporate the different gods of its subject peoples into itself provided Caesar was acknowledged as Lord. The early Christians were persecuted because they counted only Jesus as Lord; although they prayed *for* the emperor they were not prepared to pray *to* him. Under Constantine all this changed. Christianity moved from being proscribed to being official and the persecuted became the persecutors. It was Christianity that was now expected to be the religion binding the empire together and the power of the state was mobilized to make sure that this happened. The consequence of this was an immense shift in the nature of the church.

Today, without necessarily agreeing with the full scope of the Anabaptists' analysis or position, Christians would generally recognize the corrupting effect of legalization under Constantine and agree with the need to break down the concept of the sacral state. It fell to the Anabaptists actually to begin this process and to pay the price for doing so. We might wonder why the Reformers (Luther and Zwingli, in particular) drew back from their earlier radicalism and failed to carry through the reformation in a thoroughgoing way. Perhaps there are three reasons.

On a *personal level,* Luther and Zwingli had already travelled a long way and there must have been a limit to the amount of change they were personally willing to accommodate. It is one thing to imagine a different state of affairs, it is another to adapt to it.

On a *political level* to strike a blow at the state church concept with its symbol, infant and universal baptism, was to shake the established order to its foundations. The Peasants' Revolt and many other indications of national and social unrest in the ferment of the day undoubtedly caused them to draw back from being too radical too quickly. The Reformation in Germany was inextricably linked with the national aspirations of the people and the involvement of the princes in the church was an apparent necessity in shielding the new-born Reformation from anti-evangelical and anti-German forces. Luther and Zwingli were looked up to as statesmen and must have felt keenly the weight of responsibility upon them to maintain order and restrain anarchy. It was politically expedient, perhaps even responsible, to hold back. When the Anabaptists did not hold back, the hostility towards them must be seen as a fear that the social order was being altered. They were the equivalent of 'reds under the beds'.

On a *pastoral level* the Reformers were faced with the question of pace. The faster and further they went the fewer people they would be likely to persuade to go with them. Wherever change comes this same dilemma has to be faced—the radical/liberal option. Do we work for progressive change within, accommodating ourselves to the inconsistencies of the present, or do we opt for immediate and total change now? The Reformers opted for the former on the ground that the word of God had to be given time to work its work of persuading people, especially the princes. They were afraid of schism and had a horror of it. It is not that the Anabaptists were unsympathetic to this dilemma, indeed they too argued for change from within, although they were frustrated by the slow rate of change. Their dilemma was in being asked on the one hand to believe and obey the word while at the same time being asked to engage in acts such as infant baptism and the mass which their consciences told them were unbiblical. For them it was a crisis of conscience and of integrity which was to lead them to defy the established church and state. For the Anabaptists partial reformation of the institutional church was not enough. They favoured a restoration of the apostolic church, a new beginning starting with Scripture alone and following the guidelines in the Bible for the organization of the church as for the theological content of faith. The message and example of the New Testament was their binding norm and the believers' church already described was the result of their enquiries.

The love principle

The point has already been made that the Münster radicals were not representatives of the Anabaptists proper. The reason why this can be confidently asserted is to be found in the fact that the Anabaptists proper were, from the first, pacifists. The first extant writing of the Zurich radicals consists of a letter written by Conrad Grebel in September 1524 to Thomas Müntzer which, while approving of much of his teaching, takes him to task over the matter of the sword, asserting that 'the gospel and its adherents are not to be protected by the sword, nor are they thus to protect themselves . . . since all killing has ceased with them'.

The principle of love grew out of their literal observance of the sermon on the mount and their insistence upon following Christ. They refused to go to war (unlike Zwingli who died fighting in one) or to defend themselves. They refused to participate in state coercion and held that it was wrong for the followers of Jesus to do so. In expressing love, the redistribution of wealth and mutual aid were normal and some Anabaptist communities, the Hutterites, practised full-blown communal living, travelling into Moravia to find room and toleration to do so. Brotherhood came before self as far as they were concerned. These experiments were not without their blemishes or failures but were brave attempts to be faithful to Jesus, which leads us to our next point.

The centrality of Jesus

Another area where the Münster radicals were unrepresentative was in their attempt to make Old Testament social ethics, such as polygamy, normative. For the evangelical Anabaptists, important though the Bible was, it was not understood to be normative at all points. The New Testament was seen as having priority over the Old and within the New Testament Jesus was the focus. For the Anabaptists this was a crucial insight which affected their whole outlook. The state churches were able to appeal to the Old Testament to justify their institutional ideas of a church coextensive with the population. They were able to liken infant baptism to circumcision and to find a mandate for coercion in ancient Israel. The Bible was invoked to assist them in justifying their stance from a scriptural base, but only by bypassing Jesus and the New Testament. The Anabaptists understood the discontinuity between the Old and New Testaments as well as the continuity and took Jesus and the early church as their norm, ending up with a significantly different theological stance from the Reformers. While being just as evangelical, it made them also more radical and more aware of Jesus and the gospels. Their consciousness of the constant threat of martyrdom and the way of the cross served to increase their self-identification with Jesus and their awareness of what it meant to walk in his footsteps. In life and death they knew themselves to be imitators of Christ.

In this chapter, we have taken the evangelicals of Zurich as representative of what is frequently called 'the radical Reformation'. From time to time attempts have been made to trace through the history of the church an alternative 'apostolic succession', an historical descent of 'the true church' proving that however corrupt the established church might have become, the true church has survived as a church within the church. God, it has been argued, has never left himself without a witness but has preserved an apostolic community in each generation on what we might call the 'underside' of the church. In a significant book on the Anabaptists, *The Reformers and Their Stepchildren*, Leonard Verduin has argued that it is inaccurate to see the radical Reformation as the product of the Reformation. Rather, the radical Reformation was the product of forces that had long been present in the church and lay just below the surface of the medieval church ready to emerge once the lid was taken off. The Anabaptists were to be seen not as the children of the Reformers but as their stepchildren, products of other and older parents but adopted for a time by the Reformation until it became clear that the gulf was wider than at first imagined.

That there have been movements in the history of the church bearing some resemblance to the Anabaptists is not to be denied. From time to time, as the church declined from its first love and spiritual vitality, protest movements have arisen proclaiming a need to return to what once was.

In the second century Montanism, a charismatic movement with a prophetic dimension, arose as a protest against the growing worldliness and formality of the church. By 230 the group was excommunicated but not before winning Tertullian, one of the most prominent of the church's early theologians, to their ranks.

In the late third century the long development of monasticism began as a protest against the laxity of the church. Men like Antony of Egypt retired to the desert (after the pattern of John the Baptist and Jesus) to do battle with the devil and to reach out for perfection. 'Commonlife' monasticism began to develop in the fourth century as men sought for holiness in community.

The Donatist schism of the fourth century was a protest against the compromise of the Catholics during the persecutions at the beginning of the century. Their insistence on the re-baptizing of Catholic Christians led, as has been seen, to the use of the death penalty against them.

The Franciscan movement of the thirteenth century was an attempt to return to the evangelical simplicity of Christ and the early church. Later in the medieval era a series of reform movements developed; these have come to be called 'the first Reformation'. Waldensians, Hussites, Wycliffites and Bohemian Brethren developed across Europe and were suppressed until the Reformation gave them the opportunity to come into their own.

All of these movements have their similarities to the Anabaptists as do many that have emerged after the Reformation. After Münster, a Dutch priest, Menno Simons organized and led the remnants of Dutch anabaptism, bringing it back into line and giving rise to the Mennonite denominations of the present day. The Moravians continued the tradition in central Europe and new movements sprang spontaneously into life including the Puritans, the English Baptists, the early Quakers, the Brethren in Christ, the Disciples of Christ, the Plymouth Brethren and the Pentecostals.

Between many of these movements there has been a degree of continuity and interaction, but it is not possible, nor is it necessary, to prove a chain of historical causality. What these movements have in common is a *vision* which has already been called, rather inadequately, 'primitivism', the assessment of things present in the light of their own roots and origins. In the light of the New Testament theology of the church, the church has in all its ages and manifestations fallen short and been in need of restoration. It is the willingness to let this happen which is crucial.

All of these movements have been motivated by the desire to fulfil the New Testament vision of the church and in so doing to enter into a new age of spiritual vitality. The Anabaptist vision of the church is worthy of respect. In the course of time it has come to be shared by many who are not historically in the radical tradition. Most Christians are now light years away from any concept of the sacral state and would affirm the voluntary nature of faith.

The converse of this victory is the tendency of believers' churches to assume after a few generations the faults against which they originally protested. The process of institutionalization is a hard one to resist and with the removal of persecution it may be argued that the Anabaptists experienced a fall of their own into accommodation, materialism and compromise. Yesterday's radical easily becomes tomorrow's reactionary. There is no way to avoid the gravitational pull of decline other than to be caught up in a continual, though uncomfortable, tension of continuous renewal, reformation, restoration and revival. The fact that others may have failed is no excuse for us not to try.

To sustain this pilgrim, open-ended existence is the challenge of restoration. One early English separatist community in Gainsborough had it about right when they covenanted together 'to walk in all the ways of the Lord, made known *or to be made known*'. John Robinson, a leader amongst the group which became the Pilgrim Fathers echoed these sentiments in his famous words, later to be incorporated into a hymn, 'The Lord has yet more light and truth to break forth from his word.' The Anabaptists would have agreed with those words and the spirit of faith and obedience which is behind them.

3

Restoration and Experience

Pentecostalism and the charismatic experience

According to at least two major movements this century, more light and truth have indeed broken forth from God's word. In the early 1900s pentecostalism made its advent on the church scene in the wake of the Azusa Street revival in Los Angeles. For three years after 1906 people came there from all over the world to experience the outpouring or baptism of the Holy Spirit and to take back the message to their own lands. Pentecostalism, which was a movement rather than a denomination, spread rapidly, leading to the forming of new churches and the influencing—and sometimes the dividing—of existing ones. In Britain the arrival of pentecostalism coincided with the aftermath of the Welsh Revival and gathered strength from it. Worldwide pentecostalism has exerted an immense influence and is numbered today in millions.

The antecedents of pentecostalism may be traced to John Wesley and the Evangelical Revival in eighteenth-century England. Wesley was an unusual and brilliant man whose spirituality was a combination of the Anglicanism in which he had been nurtured and Moravian pietism, contact with which brought him into his 'heartwarming' experience of assurance of salvation and renewal. He was no stranger to spiritual experience and emphasized the inner witness of the Holy Spirit. It has been said that Wesley combined a strangely cool head with a strangely warmed heart. His influence upon the nation was massive. In attempting to understand the workings of the Spirit, he formulated a distinct doctrine of sanctification as a second work of grace to be distinguished from justification. Reformed theology has tended by contrast to see sanctification as a continuing process rather than a climactic work. In the wake of Wesley's doctrine, various 'holiness' movements developed in the nineteenth century stressing the importance of a second work of grace leading to the higher life. The Keswick movement was one facet of this development, preaching a second blessing which the holiness groups sometimes referred to as 'the baptism of the Holy Spirit'.

It was out of this soil that pentecostalism grew, but the newly distinctive element to emerge from the Azusa Street meetings was the notion of the baptism of the Spirit as a baptism of power rather than of holiness, and the joining of this experience with the gift of speaking in tongues. Tongues came to be seen as the initial evidence of the baptism and this remains a distinctive doctrine of pentecostalism to this day.

To understand and explain their experience, the Pentecostals employed a theology of restoration. Over the years, God had restored many facets of the apostolic church and now he was restoring the experience of baptism in the Holy Spirit and his gifts. That which was now being seen was that which had been spoken of in the book of Acts.

The initial wave of pentecostalism influenced and affected the established churches but failed to gain a foothold in them. In the early 1960s that which had previously characterized the Pentecostals, baptism in the Spirit and his gifts, began to penetrate the mainline denominations, Protestant and Catholic alike, to give rise to what was labelled initially 'neo-pentecostalism' and, more recently, 'the charismatic movement'. Christians of all traditions began to enter into a renewed experience of God in the Spirit without feeling that they were thereby obliged to secede from their denominations. The charismatic experience was accommodated to the differing theologies and structures of the churches with the result that old divisions between denominations were obscured and new divisions between those in renewal and out of it were opened up. Some of these 'renewed' believers drew upon the older Pentecostal theological models to explain their experience, but over the years there has been a far-reaching re-articulation of the meaning of charismatic experience.

The church scene of today displays an amazing variety of currents and counter-currents. Evangelicalism, once a coalition of Arminians and Calvinists, baptists and paedobaptists, is now so stretched and varied that those at opposite ends of the spectrum are scarcely able to recognize one another.

Experience

The feature which concerns us in this chapter is that both pentecostalism and charismatic renewal have been primarily movements of *experiential* renewal. The whole question of experience is firmly on the agenda for today. What should we expect to experience? How do we know that what we experience is right? How do we tell the difference between what comes from the devil, from the flesh and from the Spirit? Above all, how do we give theological expression to what we experience, and are we to preach it in such a way that others are to experience it as well?

Experience and suspicion

The problem with experience is that most of us have been taught to view it with suspicion. From early years in our Christian pilgrimage we are exhorted to ignore our feelings in favour of the facts of God's word. We are warned that our feelings might lead us astray. Feelings and faith are felt to be opposed and hostile to one another. Evangelicalism has been so orientated to the word of God that anything beyond this is immediately suspect. One of the great fears that haunts the evangelical world is the fear of 'emotionalism', of the head being ruled by the heart, of the dissipation of true religion into navel-gazing, inward-looking, self-indulgent emotionalist trivia.

It cannot be asserted that such fears are without any substance. Church history, pastoral experience and numerous anecdotes about what happened in such-and-such a church (even allowing for immense distortion) indicate that there are dangers and casualties involved in the recovery of the experiential. It is well to remember, however, that precisely this fear of excess was expressed to John Wesley by a bishop of great orthodoxy who told him, 'Enthusiasm, Mr Wesley, is a horrid thing, a most horrid thing.' It is equally good to remember the words of a later bishop of Coventry, 'Delirious emotionalism is not the chief peril of the English clergy.'

But experience has not always been regarded with such suspicion. Previous generations of evangelicals have well understood the experimental nature of Christian faith and have written extensively about it. The English Puritans, the Continental Pietists, the American Jonathan Edwards and such twentieth-century figures as A. W. Tozer have well understood Christian faith as an experiential faith in which communion with God is realized in our individual existence. They have also understood that not everything that glitters is gold, that the inevitable accompaniment of true experience of God is a new range of problems, temptations and dangers which open up before the subject of that experience, and that the presence of the counterfeit, the spurious and the excessive gather around the fringes of that experience. The price of growth in experience of God is a corresponding growth in the ability to discern and to prune away the unreal.

Christianity is without a doubt a religion of experience. It is about the work of God in regenerating the human spirit, transforming the human heart and enlightening the human mind. In Christ, the living God has drawn near to men in order that he might change and renew their lives. John is able to say, 'From the fullness of his grace we have all received one blessing after another' (Jn 1:16). Paul affirms, 'God has poured out his love into our hearts by the Holy Spirit, whom he has given us' (Rom 5:5). The New Testament abounds with words like 'new birth', 'witness' and 'anointing' which are experiential words, referring to a felt and a realized religion. The book of Acts reveals to us time and time again not a people who argued themselves into faith from an abstract base but those who encountered Christ and received the Holy Spirit and for this reason were utterly persuaded of the truth of Christianity.

The point is that experience is far more than feelings. Christian faith deals with the impact of the knowledge of God upon the spirit, soul, mind and body of the believer and therefore we must treat the inner life with the utmost seriousness.

Experience and doctrine

One of the much-voiced reservations concerning charismatic renewal has to do with the supposed priority that experience is given over doctrine. Charismatics are accused of being unbalanced in their inclination towards immediate and direct perceptions of God and away from the less immediate but more certain revelations of Scripture. The problem with this point of view is that balance, like beauty, is more often than not in the eye of the beholder. If we have been used to an imbalance away from experience, balance when it comes is apt to feel like unbalance. If many of us modern-day commentators could be miraculously transported back into the New Testament era, presumably we would be critical of the imbalance of the early church. One wonders, if we had been around on the day of Pentecost, whether we would have been among the Spirit-filled and enthusiastic or amongst those who said, making fun of them, 'They have had too much wine.' Apparently, for many, enthusiasm is all right, provided it is securely wedged between the pages of the Bible and not something with which we ourselves have to contend! To say that charismatic renewal exalts experience over truth is a misunderstanding and by and large a misplaced criticism.

It must be granted that in the history of the church there have been those who have felt at liberty to dispense with the Bible because of some supposed revelation (they are referred to in the previous chapter as 'spiritualists'). But that is not the intention, motive or effect of the vast majority of charismatic renewal which affirms the authority of the Bible as warmly as any part of the Christian constituency. What renewal does do is to highlight the *relation* between doctrine and experience. Doctrine was not and is not arrived at in a vacuum but is, itself, the product of experience and is a way of testing whether any given experience *matches* up to a certain set of experiences which are to be regarded as normative, namely the experience of Jesus, incarnate, crucified and risen as witnessed to by the apostles. In case this sounds obscure let us expand and illustrate this theme.

The New Testament did not drop out of heaven but, like the rest of the Scriptures, was the product of the experience of revelation. In Christ, the apostles and those around them experienced the presence and power of God. In the risen Christ they were confronted with one who could forgive, redeem, reconcile and transform them. They encountered Christ before they arrived at an understanding of who he was. In their hope and expectation they saw him initially as a candidate for the messiahship. To perceive this about Jesus was itself a revelation! After Peter confessed that Jesus was the Messiah, Jesus said to him, 'Blessed are you, Simon son of Jonah, for this was not revealed to you by man, but by my Father in heaven' (Mt 16:17). The revelation came to Peter in enabling him to *realize* who Jesus was and the process of realization did not cease there. Whatever Jesus may have said during his lifetime, it was not until after his resurrection that the disciples began to grasp hold of his sonship and to understand the full depth of his words. It was out of the experience of God in Christ that they began to articulate the truth that he was the Word of God who actually shared God's nature as God and had become man in order to impart the nature of God to man.

The New Testament is not a book that either originated or can be read in a vacuum. It is the deposit of the apostolic witness to Christ, the product of their experience of him. As such it occupies a normative role in the church providing us with the canon, or measuring rod, by which all other reputed experiences are to be tested. Under the influence of the Holy Spirit its witness lives again in our own experience and we encounter the Christ of whom it speaks, but it is folly to imagine that anybody who reads it comes to it without their own preconceptions or prejudices. If the revelation given us in Scripture is the product of the accumulated experience of God working in and speaking to the authors, equally my current experience, or non-experience, of God predisposes me to hear, or not to hear, certain aspects of his revelation. There is an interaction between Scripture and the reader of Scripture and the extent of this process is greater than we imagine.

Technically this process is known as 'the hermeneutical circle'. In interpreting the Bible (the discipline of 'hermeneutics') I also filter it through my own intellect, tradition, culture and personal history, and so does every person who ever reads it. There will be the subtle temptation to make it say what I want to hear, to give centrality to the themes which are important to me, and to gloss over those things which I find unacceptable or threatening. As an interpreter of Scripture I will be bringing to it the attitude of mind which I have inherited from my culture, education and intellectual assumptions. My experience of the world and my experience of God will affect the extent to which I encounter his word in Scripture. As my experience shifts, so will my interpretation. As my reading of Scripture challenges, stirs and provokes me so that my interpretation of it shifts, so my experience will shift. Scripture and experience are involved in a continuous dynamic of interpretation and it is out of this that doctrine is forged.

The point of this discussion is to expose the fact that all of us tend to read Scripture in a blinkered way and we need to acknowledge this with integrity and honesty. But in this dialogue between ourselves and Scripture (particularly the New Testament) where is the norm? What is the measuring rod whereby we test our own experience? From a restorationist point of view the answer must be that the New Testament presents us with a normative picture of what, as Christians, we should expect to experience. The alternative is to say that the New Testament is not normative, but some other standard is, in which case we have to ask what standard that is and by what authority it establishes itself. The fact is that, with regard to experience, many Christians do not accept the New Testament as normative for themselves or the church. To justify this position they erect a variety of theologies to give authority to their position.

Liberal theology

Liberal theology expressly disavows the binding authority of Scripture and sees our understanding of God in progressive, evolutionary terms. The Bible is to be interpreted in the light of the highest and the best of many insights and when this is done, there are many aspects of the early Christian witness—particularly the life of Jesus—which are seen to be superlative. There are other elements which belong to a more superstitious, non-critical and frankly supernaturalist age which saw the world in a different way from ourselves. Much that is written of in the New Testament belongs to this latter category and although it is not to be despised, neither is it to be expected or desired as part of our own experience.

Dispensational theology

Dispensationalism has the distinction of dealing with the same problem as liberal theology—viz., How are we to relate the Bible to our own day and how much of it is normative for us?—but comes to a different solution which supposedly does not reject the final authority of the Bible. The history of the world, according to this interpretation, is to be divided into a series of ages (or dispensations) in which God dealt differently with man in different ages. The New Testament belonged to one dispensation, but we live in another and therefore should not see the New Testament as applying to us in total but only in part, specifically the letters of Paul. We are clearly not to expect the manifestation in this age of that which belonged to a previous dispensation. Thus, the duty of the Christian is to defend the fact that miracles and supernatural phenomena once took place, but to deny the fact that the same should happen today. Jesus and the early church are not to be taken as being normative for the church today; they are exceptional and are to be interpreted in that way.

Evangelical theology

In reviewing this term we are using it loosely since there is no one evangelical theology. For the first half of this century there was, however, a general consensus which saw the New Testament experience of believers as being in some respects exceptional. The gifts of the Holy Spirit spoken of by Paul in 1 Corinthians 12–14 and many of the supernatural occurrences in the gospels and Acts were seen as peripheral to the work of Christ in the believer and not as essential. Jesus could perform miracles because of his deity and the miraculous accompaniments of the apostles' preaching were seen as initial phenomena contributing to the establishing of the church in its early and tender stages. Once established, the church no longer needed those signs, therefore we should not expect them today. They are at best unnecessary and at worst counterfeit. To justify this position, a series of arguments were put forward.

The exegetical argument

It has long been the custom to use 1 Corinthians 13:8–12 as the prooftext for this position and to present the argument in two forms. Paul is arguing in these verses for the primacy of love as an eternal value and he contrasts it with the limited and temporary nature of spiritual gifts. Prophecy, tongues and the gift of knowledge are all to pass away since 'when perfection comes, the imperfect disappears' (v.10).

The first variant of the argument holds that by 'perfection' Paul here means the New Testament. When the New Testament has been written and completed then there will be no need for spiritual gifts such as prophecy and tongues since the function of these gifts is to sustain the church through the early years until that which can be relied upon (God's written word) is complete and available.

As an argument this variant falls down in its understanding of what Paul means by 'perfection'. Reference to verse 12 indicates that in using this word his thoughts are not on the New Testament canon but on the coming of Jesus ('then we shall see face to face'). If this is the case, the inference would be that far from passing away, the spiritual gifts he mentions are to remain, limited and partial though they may be, until the coming of the Lord when in the fullness of his light, their partial light will be rendered unnecessary.

In coming to terms with this patently correct alternative interpretation, the exegetical argument takes on a new form in a second variant. In verse 11 Paul speaks of putting away childish things: 'When I was a child, I talked like a child, I thought like a child, I reasoned like a child. When I became a man, I put childish ways behind me.' Spiritual gifts, according to this variant, are to be seen as belonging to the spiritual immaturity which we individually and corporately need to grow out of—not return to. This explains why the Corinthian church was in such a mess—they were obsessed with the playthings of childhood. Of course, to those who understand Paul in this way, any call for the restoration of spiritual gifts sounds like a call to return to the kindergarten.

But it needs to be asked, Is this a fair interpretation of Paul? The answer must be No! Verse 11 follows logically from verse 10. Our coming of age is identified with the coming of perfection. Paul's point is that inevitably we are spiritual children and will remain so until Jesus comes. His use of the childhood image here is not a value judgement against spiritual gifts but a reminder of the limited and partial nature of so much that we are a part of. This includes our doctrines and our theologies which at his coming will be shown to be 'childlike' attempts to express the truth.

If we imagine that we are mature now, perhaps we ought to think again, or else 'that day' will be a rude awakening. Of course we are to pursue the values which endure eternally, but in this limited partial age of our spiritual youth spiritual gifts rightly used also have their place, as is demonstrated by Paul's immediate exhortation: 'Follow the way of love and eagerly desire spiritual gifts' (14:1). The prooftext approach to 1 Corinthians 13:8–12 clearly cannot carry the freight which has so often been loaded onto it. Attention therefore must turn to the second argument used to demonstrate the redundancy and therefore the illegitimacy of the spiritual gifts.

The theological argument

This is an attempt to prove what the exegetical argument failed to prove but using a broader canvas. According to this view, signs and wonders, spiritual gifts and supernatural phenomena are not to be regarded as normative for the church but as exceptional occurrences which accompany the initial stages of a new phase of revelation.

As God breaks into history, his inbreaking is accompanied by an overriding of some of the normal historical processes, thus giving rise to the miraculous. The role of the miraculous is to awaken people to God's new initiative and to confirm it; therefore the exodus—as a pivotal stage in revelation history—was accompanied by all manner of supernatural activity. Likewise the beginning of the prophetic era with Elijah and Elisha was attested by miracles and the evident presence of the supernatural. The supreme example of God's inbreaking was his own coming in Jesus and at Pentecost in the Holy Spirit. We are not to be surprised, therefore, that from beginning to end the sovereign initiative of God is marked by the supernatural, but these signs of God's coming to us are not to be seen as being normative. They are clearly exceptional and we ask wrongly if we ask for them to be reproduced, since God's revelatory initiatives are now complete.

The theological argument is right in its analysis but wrong in its deduction. It is manifestly and gloriously true that the initiating work of God is accompanied by the miraculous, but it is wrong to deduce that *therefore* the miraculous has no continuing place in the ongoing life of the church. It is possible to agree with the basic analysis presented here without following through with the deduction. The evidence we have, the New Testament, would suggest that the aftermath of the dramatic inbreaking of God on the day of Pentecost was not the cessation of supernatural phenomena but (a) the periodic dramatic inbreaking of God into new groups of people (such as the Samaritans and Cornelius's household) and (b) the continuance of signs and spiritual gifts as a normative part of church life, albeit on a reduced scale. The Corinthian church witnesses to this despite its aberrations.

Against the theological argument advanced here it may be averred that nowhere does the New Testament suggest that the spiritual phenomena of the early church are for a limited duration. Indeed Paul, even while correcting the Corinthians, affirms them in their desire for spiritual gifts. He takes the significant step of linking spiritual gifts to the existence of the church as the body of Christ (1 Cor 12), the logic of which is that as long as the church exists as Christ's body on earth, the manifestation of spiritual gifts will be found within it.

Before considering a further argument which would question whether we can take the New Testament as normative for our experience it would be good to consider what it is that the liberal, the dispensational and the traditional evangelical views have in common. All these views are reluctant to allow that the experience of the early Christians should be taken as normative for ourselves.

The liberal view makes no secret of the fact that the New Testament is not binding or normative save in so far as we allow it to be. We may not agree with this position but it does have integrity and is an honest position. The dispensational and evangelical positions agree with the liberal in denying the normative status of the New Testament for experience, but do so while continuing to assert the authority of Scripture.

The dispensationalist does this by erecting over Scripture a theological grid which enables him to assert that Scripture is true but not normative. He thus comes to the same conclusion as the liberal by a different route. The strength of the dispensational view is that it is clear, simple and secure (which accounts for its popularity). Its fundamental weakness is that, although there is a measure of support within Scripture for the idea of 'dispensations' (as in 2 Cor 3:7–18), dispensationalism is a man-made theological system which actually deflects us from encountering God in his word and which simultaneously both asserts the authority of Scripture in theory and denies it for us in practice.

The traditional evangelical position does not escape this criticism since it too denies that the New Testament gives us a norm for experience. However, it does so not by erecting a system. Instead it enunciates a theological principle which in itself is not derived from Scripture but from the gulf which separates our experience from New Testament experience, namely the assumption that certain phenomena of the early church were for the duration of the apostolic period only.

When it is obvious that we do not experience today what was experienced in the early church, it is a natural deduction that what happened then must have been for them but not for us. Unfortunately, it is the wrong deduction since it makes our experience normative over the New Testament and therefore requires that the New Testament should be accommodated to us and not we to it. We must beware of theologizing our non-experience in order to avoid the challenge of actually submitting ourselves to the authority of God's word.

The restorationist claim, in distinction from these views, is that what we see in Jesus and in the early church represents what God wants to do in each of us and in the church. The humanity of Jesus is normative humanity. His mighty acts are not to be attributed to his deity (and therefore limited to him) but to his sanctified humanity. So, by his Spirit and in his name, we are capable of doing what he did. Jesus taught us as much when he said, "I tell you the truth, anyone who has faith in me will do what I have been doing. He will do even greater things than these because I am going to the Father. And I will do whatever you ask in my name, so that the Son may bring glory to the Father. You may ask me for anything in my name, and I will do it' (Jn 14:12–14). In the church today, therefore, we need to stop rationalizing our inexperience and then finding good theological reasons to justify it: we need to be restored. At this point we can approach the third stand of the evangelical argument.

The experiential argument

Our dilemma is that, even if an exegetical and theological case can be made out for the restoration of spiritual gifts, we are still left with the need to prove that what purports to be the same category of experience as in New Testament times is in fact so. How do we know that what is claimed to be the restoration of New Testament experience is actually the same as that to which the New Testament bears testimony? In short, how do we know that the gift of tongues which is experienced today is the same as that which was known in the New Testament, or that any of the spiritual gifts which are claimed are the same as in the early church?

As an example, let us take the New Testament experience of healing. The form of healing evidenced in Jesus and the apostles is nearly always one of instantaneous and direct healing. Yet the experience of healing in the church today is by and large only partially successful. Only a proportion of those prayed for are healed and an even smaller number of these are healed instantaneously. How can it be claimed that the New Testament gift of healing has been restored if the results do not match up?

Each of the reputed spiritual gifts might similarly be analysed and found to fall short of the New Testament evidence. Evidence in plenty could be amassed to instance cases where the interpretation of tongues missed the point, or where 'words of knowledge' were wildly astray, or where 'prophecies' did not come to pass. In this way it is possible to reduce the 'success rate' of charismatic gifts to a point where the residue of successes can be explained in terms of chance, guesswork or psychosomatic healing.

Admitting that there is some truth in this kind of analysis, what interpretation of it can be offered? The most obvious and extreme viewpoint is simply to ascribe all charismatic phenomena to the work of the devil. At least this view has the merit of being straightforward, but those who hold it must be hard put to explain how so many Christians—including many mature, fruitful, educated and godly believers —have been led astray.

A more charitable, although less straightforward view, is to understand present-day charismatic phenomena in terms of man's subconscious and intuitive being; thus speaking in tongues, although it may not be the same gift as evidenced in the New Testament, is nevertheless a form of non-verbal self-expression which when claimed and sanctified by the Holy Spirit is helpful to those who choose to use it—provided they do not get it out of focus and provided they understand that others might find it quite unhelpful. One man's meat can be another man's poison, even in spiritual terms, so it seems. The same approach may be applied to healing and any other gifts—they are valuable and valid for some though not to be understood as a restoration, but as a reclaiming of the intuitive dimensions of our being in the service of God.

This approach has a number of advantages. Firstly, it attempts to take seriously the psychological dimension of spiritual phenomena. As with any other human experience it is possible to attempt a psychological description of the experience of spiritual gifts. The fact that one can, for instance, describe conversion in psychological terms does not mean that it is not also a spiritual act or process. Instead it is a psychological description of the effect of spiritual influence. So it should also be possible to attempt a description of what is happening psychologically when a person speaks in tongues or prophesies.

Secondly, the person who holds this view is able to relate positively to charismatics without feeling either that he must deny the validity of their experience on the one hand or that he must necessarily fall in with it and become a charismatic himself on the other. Charismatic and non-charismatic expressions of theology and life are equally valid from this perspective.

The problem with this viewpoint, however, is the old one of eating your cake and having it. The only question with which we have to deal at the end of the day is, Is God at work in charismatic renewal or is he not? If he is not then I have no choice but to resist it. If he is then I have no choice but to throw my lot in with it. This is not to deny that charismatic renewal is a reclaiming of the total dimensions of human nature and that the analysis here presented, which recognizes the role of intuition and the subconscious is valid, but it is to say that charismatic renewal cannot be reduced to this level. Man's intuitive nature is the arena for the operation of the Spirit, as are other dimensions of our being.

A third point of view, that taken by the restorationist himself, is as follows. The claim is not that the New Testament experience of spiritual gifts has been restored *in toto* but that it is capable of being restored, that it should be restored and that at this point of time it is in process of being restored. Whatever discrepancies are evident in the current experience of these things are therefore to be attributed to the partial understanding which prevails at this point of the ongoing pilgrimage. It is not to be expected that we will attain to the level of competence of Jesus and the apostles easily or speedily. The apostles themselves had to learn, and on at least one notable occasion completely failed in their ministry to one demonized boy. They were frequently taken to task by Jesus because of their unbelief and trained in the practical school of faith. Jesus himself was limited in what he could do in his home town because of the failure of the people to honour him and to believe in him. If this is the case with Jesus and the apostles, it should be no surprise that the church today, which has made unbelief into a fine art, should need to *learn* the nature and function of spiritual gifts and the quality of faith through which they become operative.

Neither should the fact that there is still much to learn deflect us from the many very genuine and real benefits that have been received—authentic and lasting healings, clear and edifying prophetic utterances, gifts of knowledge, wisdom and discernment beyond that which is humanly possible, and many other things. It is no accident that nationally and internationally the church is growing fastest where the cutting edge of spiritual gifts is in evidence, because spiritual gifts are tools for the building of Christ's body. The important thing in discerning and understanding experience is not to put it under the microscope but to perceive in whose name it comes, whom it seeks to glorify and what the fruits of it are.

If antipathy to the restoration of the full dimensions of New Testament experience does not have its origin in accurate exegesis or in sound theology, where does it come from? The answer to that is found in the forces which have shaped western theology in its attitude of mind. The fact is that intellectualism has been the dominant force in western evangelical Christianity for some centuries, and, looked at from one aspect, charismatic renewal is a breaking free from the dominant one-dimensional form of Christian experience to replace it with an approach which affirms the reality of God in all the dimensions of our being. This is to be perceived in the nature of charismatic worship which allows of bodily forms of worship and expression (clapping, dancing, raising hands) and of intuitive perceptions of God in the spirit (expressed through spiritual gifts) as opposed to the word-heavy, intellectual approach to worship which has until recently prevailed.

The hostility to the renewal and restoration of spiritual gifts is not so much rooted in biblical and theological concerns as in fear of its implied break with the security of intellectualism, where the concern is more with analysis than with action. What passes under the guise of sound theology is more often than not a form of western rationalism which has no room for the supernatural and suprarational activity of God and which has been learnt from the world.

The theologies which see the New Testament as exceptional and not normative for our experience are attempts to rationalize our non-experience and find a theology for it. The alternative is to engage in a costly recasting of our ways of thinking and of our expectations. Western Christianity, by and large, has been used to charting the sea of faith in intellectual terms but has not learnt to do so adequately in experiental terms and has sought to rationalize its inadequacy into a theology. Over against this, the restorationist claim is to provoke the church to recover the totality of New Testament experience.

J. I. Packer is right to say, 'The central charismatic quest is not for any particular experience as such, but for what we may call thoroughgoing and uninhibited totality in realising God's presence and responding to his grace.' (*Keep in Step with the Spirit*, page 231.)

4

Restoration and the Structures of the Church

Salvation and society

The Christian faith is intensely personal. It deals with the value, the redemption and the sanctification of men and women. It asserts that in the plan of God, God has known us and loved us by name since before all time. His plan is worked out by the calling of individual men and women to respond to Christ and to know him. The individual walk of the Christian believer is given much time and attention in Scripture and rightly so since the church is the gathering of those who have been called. If so far in this book the focus has largely been given to the church, it is not to deny that the church is rooted in the individual.

To remain healthy the church must stress the place and responsibility of the individual, and in seeing the corporate we should not lose sight of the individual. However, if there has been a tendency in the last few hundred years it has been towards individualism rather than corporatism.

In the mind of the church, individuals have been stressed to the detriment of the corporate. No doubt this has its origin in the Reformation's strong focus upon the need for the individual to be justified by faith and the recovery of the correspondingly personal nature of salvation. It is evidenced in the basic assumption of the evangelical church that its main task is that of personal evangelism—to persuade people to decide for Jesus now and thus to go to heaven in due course—and in its belief that social change is to be brought about by the moral transformation of sufficient numbers of individuals.

While no Christian can deny that 'the heart of the human problem is the problem of the human heart', is it truly biblical or realistic to imagine that this is an adequate understanding of the human predicament or of the full scope of salvation? How do we come to terms with the fact, for instance, that in many situations where there is a high density of born again Christians, large-scale social injustice not only exists but appears to be supported by the evangelical population? In the United Kingdom, Northern Ireland contains a higher proportion of evangelicals than practically any other part of the country and yet is riddled with deeper and worse social unrest than any other part. It is clearly true that behind that unrest lie many factors of culture, identity and history but it is also true that the religious factor—indeed the evangelical factor—is a major contribution to the division of Northern Irish society, that evangelicals are amongst the most aggressive in the statement of their views and that fear of Rome is part of their problem. What effect would large-scale conversions have upon the social problem? Would this make for peace or otherwise?

Or take South Africa as another example. The white community is marked by a high level of commitment to evangelical religion. The roots of white communities (particularly of the Afrikaners) are in Calvinistic Protestantism. Those who are upholders of the apartheid system (surely a gross denial of the Christian view of man) are often strong churchmen. Some at least of the apologetic for separate development makes its appeal to the Scriptures. No doubt in their personal lives, those who support apartheid are for the most part honourable, honest and moral people. They may be very kind to their black acquaintances. But a system which in practice means the oppression of many human beings by others, is being supported and even justified by Christian people. It must be clear that an individual conversion which enables us to go on supporting a corrupt system, albeit in a more honest and 'Christian' way than before, is somehow inadequate.

We could talk of other countries too. South Korea and many South American nations now have large Christian populations but social injustice and social evil still flourish. In these cases it may be objected that the cumulative effect of individual conversion has yet to have its full impact on society, that it takes time for the fruit of social righteousness to grow out of the stump of individual transformation. Both these points would be true. But they do not account for South Africa or Northern Ireland where the Christian roots are strong, the Christian presence is considerable and the overt evangelical stance appears to belong more to the problem than to the solution. Why has not individual conversion proved adequate?

The radical answer to this is that individual transformation is only part of God's solution to the human dilemma. Without that individual transformation there is no solution, but because there is more to the problem there must be more to the answer. The problem is that evil is corporate as well as individual. Individuals, even those who are Christians, are caught up in the grip of social, economic and cultural forces which render them unfree. A solution is needed on this level as well as on the personal level. There is structural evil enshrined in the very fabric of our corporate life as well as personal evil.

When we examine the proclamation of Jesus we find that his message was not the egocentric, salvation technique appealing to man's self-interest which it has become in much modern evangelism. He was not primarily concerned with offering people a way to heaven. He proclaimed the kingdom of God. Indeed, there was—and still is—an individual response to that kingdom namely repentance. But the kingdom itself is a new order displacing the old order and embracing both the individual and corporate dimensions of human life. We need a restoration of this full-orbed gospel of the kingdom in our understanding, preaching and living.

In due course we will attempt to understand how the kingdom of God relates to the corporate structures of both the church and society. To lay the foundations for this it is necessary to spend some time establishing a biblical analysis of the corporate. It is for the want of such an understanding that we have been led into individualism. The analysis of the individual's need and of the effect of sin upon him has been well understood within the church, leading to a confident personal application of the gospel. Not so with the corporate. Marxism has sprung into this vacuum with its critique of social history as an interaction between the material vested interests of different groups within society. It is tempting to imagine what might have happened if at the Reformation—or subsequently—there had been an adequate Christian analysis of society which had gained normative status. As we have seen, however, it was at this point that Luther capitulated to necessity and the status quo.

Christ and 'the powers'

The radical discipleship school offers such an analysis. In doing so it draws upon the Pauline teaching on the subject of principalities and powers as reassessed in the 1950s by Hendrik Berkhof in his small book *Christ and the Powers* and as further developed by John Howard Yoder in his book *The Politics of Jesus*.

Drawing neither upon Marxism nor upon current sociological theory, Berkhof seeks to lay bare what Paul had in mind when referring to 'the powers'. It might be accurately asserted that this re-examination was prompted by the events that shook Christian Europe during the Nazi era, where the state took on demonic proportions.

When Paul refers variously in the epistles to principalities, powers, thrones, dominions, elemental spirits (translated as 'basic principles of the world' in the NIV, e.g. Gal 4:3; Col 2:8, 20) the tendency has been to assume either that he is using outworn and outdated mythological language that we can safely ignore—the stance of liberal theologians—or that he is referring exclusively to the hierarchy of evil, the supernatural powers of darkness with which we are in continual spiritual warfare—the usual evangelical interpretation.

Without (on the whole) wanting to reduce or deny this latter understanding, the radical discipleship school offers a somewhat different understanding. The principalities and powers to which Paul refers are to be understood as the basic structures of human life. They are the forces which make for the regularity, system and order of human society and history. They may be understood, according to John Howard Yoder (*The Politics of Jesus*, page 145), as

> religious structures (especially the religious undergirdings of stable ancient and primitive societies), intellectual structures ('ologies and 'isms), moral structures (codes and customs), political structures (the tyrant, the market, the school, the courts, race, and nation).

As he says, 'The totality is overwhelmingly broad.'

Yoder makes several further points concerning these powers.

1) These structures were *created by God* (Col 1:15–17) and therefore may be conceived of in their essence as part of a good creation. We cannot live without them. In God's creative plan their purpose was to serve and enhance human life and society. In their nature these powers are an example of the whole being greater than the sum of the parts. It is this 'more' which is the 'power'. They are real entities, yet without man they would have no substance in the same way as a marriage is more than a man and a woman yet would not exist apart from them.

2) Like man, these powers have *rebelled and are fallen*. They

are therefore not conformed to God's original purpose. Instead of serving man they enslave him by losing their modesty and their servant status and claiming for themselves an absolute value. They have claimed the status of idols and have succeeded in making man serve them as if they were of absolute importance.

3) Despite their fallenness the powers are *still subject to the providential sovereignty of God*. He is still able to use them for good. Although they enslave men they are still necessary to man. It is within these structures that man has been preserved and that he awaits the redeeming power of God. Yoder affirms (page 146):

> Far from being archaic or meaningless, the 'exousiology' of the Apostle, i.e. his doctrine of the Powers, reveals itself to be a very refined analysis of the problems of society and history, far more refined than the other ways in which theologians have sought to describe the same realities in terms only of 'creation' or 'personality'.

Such an analysis also provides the perspective from which the radical is able to view the established order and to provide the following overview.

1) The human problem is to be understood in terms of *man's rebellion against God and his consequent alienation from his creator,* from himself, from others and from nature. Man lives in a theological-psychological-sociological-ecological dischord which accounts for his plight. A consequence of his estrangement from God is the corresponding estrangement of the powers created by God to serve and enhance man's existence. These religious, intellectual, moral and political structures have, in the discord and fragmentation of a fallen world, assumed a momentum of their own. They are not conformed to God's purpose. Man needs them to give order and shape to his existence but is at the same time enslaved and oppressed by them. They seek to be autonomous and self-important. They are boastful and self-aggrandizing. Thus man's problem and dilemma is both personal and cor-

porate. He needs to be freed from his guilt, from the power of sin and from the powers that enslave him.

2) Having understood the powers in terms of the structures of human existence, as that which is produced when the whole is more than the sum of its parts, what relation does this bear to *the demonic*? Is this understanding of principalities and powers an attempt to demythologize the New Testament teaching on the reality of Satan and the demonic? Emphatically not. In this book the reliability of the New Testament witness to the demonic is accepted without hesitation. It must be remembered that the radical discipleship movement is deeply biblical in its inspiration and orientation; it is fundamentally evangelical. The reality of the demonic cannot be reduced merely to a sociological entity. But if we are understanding Paul correctly we should see that there is a continuum between the powers and the demonic. Because the powers are fallen and autonomous they become the areas in which the demonic may exercise its oppressive power over the affairs of man. This is why Paul does not overtly attempt to distinguish between what we would call (although Paul would not) the 'natural' and the 'supernatural'. For him the whole oppressive system against which the church wrestles, merges into one whole.

3) Whereas God ultimately intends to destroy the devil and his angels, it is his purpose *to reconcile the powers to himself.* God's intention is to restore everything in the created order which has been estranged: 'He made known to us the mystery of his will according to his good pleasure, which he purposed in Christ, to be put into effect when the times will have reached their fulfilment—to bring all things in heaven and on earth together under one head, even Christ' (Eph 1:9–10).

The work of Jesus in his living, dying and rising has made this possible. When Jesus came he lived as a free man. He was subject to the powers but not bound by them. When he died it was because the powers represented by Jewish religion and Roman politics conspired against him and crucified him. He challenged their rule and they responded accordingly. According to Yoder (page 148):

> Here we have for the first time to do with a man who is not the slave of any power, of any law or custom, community or institution, value or theory. Not even to save his own life will he let himself be made a slave of these Powers.

Thus when Jesus rose from the grave, being vindicated by God, he broke the sovereignty of the powers. 'And having disarmed the powers and authorities, he made a public spectacle of them, triumphing over them by the cross' (Col 2:15). He proved and demonstrated that their rule was at an end, that they must and will yield to the sovereignty of the King. As Berkhof says:

> The concrete evidence of this triumph is that at the cross Christ has 'disarmed' the Powers. The weapon from which they heretofore derived their strength is struck out of their hands. This weapon was the power of illusion, their ability to convince men that they were the divine regents of the world . . . Unmasked, revealed in their true nature, they have lost their mighty grip on men. The cross has disarmed them: wherever it is preached, the unmasking and the disarming of the Powers takes place. (Quoted in Yoder, pages 149–50.)

4) The perspective gained in the above enables us to understand *the role of the church*. The role of the church is to do what Jesus did, to be the agent of the kingdom of God. It is to refuse to be enslaved to the powers, to remain free and to proclaim the new order in which all things are to yield to Jesus Christ as Lord. The church's proclamation centres upon the cross which is where Christ has destroyed the hold of Satan over mankind, reconciled men and women to God by averting their guilt and triumphed over the powers. It is aimed at reconciling individuals to God and enabling them to live as those to whom Jesus Christ is truly Lord. It is aimed at dethroning everything—class, state, religion—which pretends to be a rival to him.

The church and 'the powers'

How this perspective can be worked out in the social sphere we shall see in due course. Our concern now should be to apply it to the theme of restoration and the structures of the church. If the church of Christ is to fulfil its mission it must keep itself free from the seductive influence of the powers. All that is true of the powers—the tendency towards self-exaltation, self-importance and self-aggrandizement—is as true of ecclesiastical structures as it is of anything else. The same dynamic is at work. When we remain true to the first principle of restoration and examine the ecclesiastical system which we call the church against the New Testament revelation the disparity is absolutely amazing. What we call the church has more in common with the system of religion which crucified Jesus than with Jesus himself.

Entirely contrary to the teaching of Jesus the church has amassed for itself great wealth, it has established hierarchies which are parallel to the command structures of worldly organizations, it has concerned itself with titles which focus attention on man, which relate to their importance and position, it has attached importance to robes and clothing which draw attention to the academic status and achievements of the wearers, it has established a career structure with overtones of prestige and position.

We have already seen that the Anabaptists spoke of the legalization of the church by Constantine as the 'fall' of the church. Once recognized as the religion of the empire the church then began to fulfil the requirements of the empire and became corrupt. It must be evident to any simple reader of the New Testament how far this corruption has gone. The church, which was called into being to be the contradiction of the world's ways, has become its mirror image. The church has become enslaved to the powers and needs to break free.

Of course, within the church there have always been pinpricks of light and life. Within its structures have been very many who have lived with Christ and reflected him, and from time to time the restoration of the New Testament vision has given birth to renewal movements within and beyond the established church structures. But even here the same phenomenon is to be noticed. Movements which in their initial impulse have burned with energy and vitality and which have displayed a charismatic anointing of the Holy Spirit have within a generation or two grown stale and have ossified, needing then to be renewed themselves. Some of them in their turn have spawned and then ejected renewal movements. Many of them today resemble precisely those hardened institutionalized structures against which originally they were a protest.

Time and time again the church has witnessed a recapitulation of the last weeks of Jesus' life. The Messiah has come with a lowly heart to the temple which was rightly his, but those who had taken charge of the temple and were using it for their own commercial and religious ends have, for religious reasons, refused to accept his authority and have cast him out. Time and time again the words of Jesus have proven true: 'And no-one pours new wine into old wineskins. If he does, the wine will burst the skins, and both the wine and the wineskins will be ruined. No, he pours new wine into new wineskins' (Mk 2:22). The hardened wineskins of institutional Judaism were unable to cope with the fermenting new wine of the kingdom of God and that perennial tendency of the church's institutional forms to become hard and inflexible has bedevilled the church ever since. This is true both outside and inside the individual congregation. The antipathy of the church's hierarchical systems to renewing movements of the Holy Spirit is more than equalled by the resistance within congregations to that same work. As many a pastor knows to his cost, the experience of a renewal can be a delightful springtime until the church's internal institutional forms are threatened with change.

What is happening in all of this? The ecclesiastical powers

are being dethroned and are countering with resistance. There is an inner dynamic momentum which is inherent in the institutional structures of our fallen world. Once established those structures assert themselves. They see themselves as being self-existent. They demand attention and influence simply because they are. They require loyalty to themselves and lose sight of their intended aim. What was intended to serve the kingdom becomes a point of vested interest which resists the kingdom. Change which threatens their existence or diminishes their importance is resisted. They gather to themselves servants who are like them and the church is slowly transformed from being a place where Christ rules to being a place where the powers rule. Vast amounts of time, money and effort of devoted Christian labours are spent servicing institutional forms which do not in the event serve God's kingdom. It is here that we can see the cleverness of a demonic strategy to divert us from the real task.

The restoration movement and institutional change

The 'house-church movement' has arisen on the scene against this backdrop. Its inspiration is the restoration emphasis of returning to our scriptural roots to see what we should be doing and how we should be doing it. Its focus in the first years of its life has tended to be on the structures of the church. It has raised questions concerning the internal life of the local church and the nature of translocal ministries. It has claimed that apostles and prophets are active in the church today and that their ministry is vital for the maturing of the church. It has caused a fluttering in the ecclesiastical dovecotes because it has appeared radical and—even worse—successful. Yet, if the pessimistic picture already sketched in this chapter concerning the perpetual cycle of institutional atrophy is to be changed, it is absolutely essential to hear what God is saying through this phenomenon and to work out its implications even if this means far-reaching, costly and painful institutional change. What has it to say?

We need to see that this movement, which from now on I shall call the restoration movement, does not speak with one voice. It is shaped by a variety of forces. Out of the original impetus of the charismatic movement a general thrust towards a new form of church life developed in the early 1970s. Many of those new forms were initially worked out in house-church situations; others have evolved out of institutional churches. Some groups have deliberately avoided purchasing premises and have relied on hired halls. Other groups as a matter of policy have sought to 'tool up' for their task and have acquired and renovated buildings, usually to a very high standard.

In the late 1970s and early 1980s distinct groups within the restoration movement began to emerge more clearly. The distinguishing marks tend to derive from the distinctive teachings, the personality and style of the leading members of each group. Between some groups there is disagreement. Some restoration churches maintain a degree of separateness from any group, others draw from several. Some are suspicious and critical towards denominational churches, others less so. Thus part of the difficulty in speaking of the restoration movement lies in the fact that at many points what is true of some is not true of all.

The restoration movement does not speak with one voice but it does speak the same language. It is the language of thorough obedience. In its perception the work of renewal, although good, is not of itself enough. Where it leaves unbiblical practices unchanged it is considered to be incomplete. New wine requires new wineskins and renewal must be accompanied by the restoration of the New Testament principles of church life. These include a regenerate church membership, believers' baptism, leadership by elders, church discipline and the recognition of translocal apostolic and prophetic ministries.

Some restoration leaders believe that charismatic renewal has waned because it has stopped short of the cost involved in making changes in these areas. Of the proposed changes many are already widely accepted within the church. The believers' church, believers' baptism and eldership concepts, although seen as radical when first revived, are now extremely widely practised throughout the universal church and have made inroads into the very institutional churches which initially opposed them. They are referred to elsewhere in this book and will be covered in more detail at those points. However, one of the most controversial newer developments has been the restatement of the concept of apostleship which until recently was firmly confined by most denominations to the New Testament era. As this is a fundamental issue, from all points of view, much of the remainder of this chapter will concentrate on it.

The restoration movement and apostleship

I believe that, within a few years, references to apostolic ministries within the church will seem as acceptable and as natural as references to elders. From the restoration perspective, which sees the New Testament as the normative revelation, if it should seem right to expect the restoration to the church of New Testament gifts, why should we not also expect the restoration of New Testament ministries?

There is no way, of course, in which the original twelve apostles can ever or will ever be restored. In choosing the replacement for Judas—Matthias—Peter outlined the necessary qualifications. He was to have been with Jesus from the time of John's baptism until the ascension and was to have been a witness of the resurrection (Acts 1:21–22). The apostles were the companions of Jesus and witnesses to the resurrection and are thus historically unrepeatable. They were apostles with a big 'A'. But the New Testament bears witness to a wider apostolic function which was not confined to the twelve. The work of pioneering, church planting, laying of foundations, leadership oversight and problem solving was engaged in by others than the twelve, including

Paul, Apollos, Adronicus and Junias, Titus, Silas, Timothy and Barnabas, all of whom are explicitly referred to as apostles at various points in the New Testament. It appears to be possible to distinguish between the apostleship of Christ, the apostleship of the original twelve and the broader band of working apostles to whom reference is made.

Acts 13 gives us a model of how such apostleship could have been recognized and mobilized as it describes the calling and commissioning of Saul and Barnabas, by the Holy Spirit through the church at Antioch. Understood in this way, the claim to apostleship is not an egotistical claim that there is a special, limited edition of super-leaders with super-authority, of whom Brother X is one and so am I. It is simply a job description. It is the recognition of a needed function within the church—that at least is the significance and the flow of Ephesians 4:11–16 where apostles along with other ministries are given to enable the church to come to maturity and to fulfil its mission.

It is possible to look at the apostleship issue from different angles. Reference has already been made to the biblical angle. Looked at *historically* the expectation that some form of 'apostolic' ministry would continue in the church has been relatively constant in the church. Although obscurity surrounds the origin of the episcopacy, and the exact nature of the transition from apostleship to episcopacy is unclear, it is evident that bishops were intended to fill the oversight gap in the ongoing church. The concept of apostolic succession, although at odds with the ethos of this book, indicates an historical awareness of an ongoing apostolic ministry. Even in free churches a wider ministry of oversight has been established, as for instance the area superintendent among Baptists, the superintendent minister among Methodists, and the moderator in the United Reformed Church. Each of these roles must find its biblical rationale in the dimension of apostolic ministry to which the New Testament bears witness. Why should it seem outrageous if the restoration movement pursues a similar impulse, yet simply chooses to use the word the Bible itself uses? Historically there is a close analogy to this present-day phenomenon among the Baptists of the late seventeenth and early nineteenth centuries. Groups of churches set aside some of their more competent ministers as 'messengers' (their translation of the word *apostolos*) to pioneer new churches, oversee existing ones and to exercise a caring ministry towards other pastors. This was a ministry within the church born of the needs of the church.

When viewed *practically* it can be seen that churches (such as those which comprise the restoration movement) which are not coming from an institutional hierarchical background will have an impetus to seek some form of relationship with senior, competent and tested ministers who can give direction to the churches and care for their leaders. In other words they will seek some kind of input which may broadly be described as 'apostolic'. The major difference between this and similar structures in the denominational churches is that it is organic rather than organizational, and charismatic rather than institutional. Whereas it may well be objected that this leaves too much room for excess, extremes and eccentricity to emerge in these ministries, it can equally be claimed that ecclesiastical institutions, with their tendency to be autonomous and self-aggrandizing powers, have their own corrupting influence. Such institutions will tend to recruit men in these positions who serve the interest of the organization rather than the kingdom. They will assess men on the basis of their education and loyalty rather than on their spirituality. They will avoid the radical in favour of the mediocre. They will mistake ecclesiastical authority for spiritual authority.

The case for apostolic ministries to arise organically and charismatically within the church is a strong one. The need is stronger still.

In stating the case for the recovery of some expression of apostolic ministry, we also need to be aware that there are significant differences between the early church and ourselves which will affect the way apostleship is understood.

We are no longer in the pioneering situation, at least in this country, in which the New Testament apostles found themselves. They were preaching Christ where he had never previously been named, we are preaching him where he has been named for centuries and therefore cannot be pioneers in that sense, however adventurous or enterprising we might be. If there is an apostolic ministry in the church in this country today it will inevitably have the character of oversight of settled situations to a degree that New Testament apostles did not, since they were always geographically pushing forward the frontiers of mission and were therefore unable to remain for a long time in any situation.

In the light of this fact, the transition from apostles to bishops in the sub-apostolic era is of interest since this appears to reflect a transition from pioneering apostolic ministries to a more settled bishoping ministry exercised towards established congregations. Perhaps what are being rediscovered in the restoration movement as apostolic ministries are in fact better described as forms of charismatic and non-institutional 'bishoping' to which there are parallels in some of the Mennonite communities of the USA.

In my view the best way to approach the issue of apostles is to speak of the need the church has for a translocal, apostolic dimension in its life—a level of ministry and input which is broader than the more local ministry of the pastor-teacher. We should be careful not to legislate about how this apostolic dimension should be provided. In some cases it may be filled by one person, in other cases by several persons with differing contributions. Not all those functioning in the apostolic dimension will have the same capacity. Some will fill it more adequately than others, although none will fill it completely since no one is omnicompetent. In some cases it may be that congregations exercise an apostolic ministry towards others without this necessarily being focused in any one individual and without this implying domination of one congregation by another. The dimension of apostolic ministry is necessary, but exactly how it is fulfilled may vary and we should avoid rigid expectations of how it should be. In addition, as we shall see, there is a major difference between seeing this apostolic role as a servant ministry which acts as an enabling resource for the local church and seeing it as a ruling ministry exercising authority over it.

Pitfalls for the restoration movement

The next chapters will pursue further themes raised by the radical witness of the restoration movement. In concluding the present chapter, three areas need to be touched on which indicate danger points for the movement.

There is the danger of *structuralism,* that is an undue focus on the way the church is organized rather than where it stands with God. It is of the nature of structures that they tend to assume undue prominence. We imagine that when we have got everything organized properly with our house groups, elders and apostles all in place we will somehow be especially pleasing to God. In all of us there is an egotistical tendency which wants to be identified with something that looks good, and it leads towards Pharisaism, a preoccupation with external appearance rather than inward reality. In the drive to establish a perfect, spotless church we can miss the point that God deposits his treasure in earthen vessels. The temptation to navel gaze can divert us from actually doing the job he has given us to do.

If our focus is upon structures rather than on Christ we are bound to end up in legalism and externalism. What is needed in the era of structures is a healthy dose of pragmatism. No structures are commanded as essential—the important thing is doing the job and fulfilling the mission rather than an obsession with correctness. The New Testament indicates that the early Christians were prepared to work with what they were presented with rather than be fastidious about the right way of doing things.

There is the danger of *scholasticism*. Having understood the place of apostolic ministries and having received fresh insights into the nature and ordering of the church, the temptation is then to *over-define* the way these things should work. Precise expectations are then spelt out which go beyond the Scriptures and attempts are made to legislate for the church. We imagine we have discovered *the* way of doing things and everybody else should follow suit. But God does not work like that. Having defined our position we can then find that we are barren. God has an infinite variety of ways of working. As Paul and Apollos and Peter were different men exercising their apostolic ministry differently, so God proceeds to produce a variety which defies our neat systems. He raises up different kinds of apostolic ministries relating to different churches in different ways with different values. Rather than judge one another to see whether what is happening elsewhere makes the grade, we do better to think and speak modestly and to look to Christ rather than for conformity.

Finally, there is the danger of *denominationalism*. The suggestion that the various streams of restoration churches are in fact setting up new denominations is one which their critics like to make and which they themselves dislike hearing. Yet what makes a denomination? Is it external structure or internal attitudes? On the basis of observable history, we need to assert that there has not been and never will be any radical movement in the history of the church which is not subject to precisely the same dangers as those found in the very structures against which they are a protest. The same tendencies towards self-assertion, self-protection and self-aggrandizement will be there also, and eternal vigilance is necessary to keep free from becoming enmeshed in them. It is an impulse inherent in any institutional form to look for prestige, recognition, influence and power, and much wisdom is needed if these things are to be avoided. Whether this can be done in the restoration movement has yet to be seen.

5
Restoration and Authority

Authority, delegated authority and submission

A basic perspective of this book is that the so-called house-church movement is a modern-day expression of a persistent vision which has an honourable pedigree in the history of the church—the vision of a church restored according to the pattern of New Testament teaching. As with previous such restorationist movements, the phenomenon is a diverse one and not all the current restorationist streams (of which there are a number) are identical. Some are stricter, more disciplined and more conscious of authority than others; they take a harder line on the 'correct' style of church life and consequently are more critical of others, especially established denominational churches. Other house-church streams, while operating with a similar overall theology, are more easygoing, more expansive, more tolerant and less authority-conscious.

No charge against the house-church movement has been so often repeated as that of being authoritarian. Scare stories abound of how this authoritarianism has been applied, and of the casualties of it. Honesty and charity require it to be acknowledged that there has been a gross amount of distortion in this area. Even Christians can be keen to hear the worst of others and we all know how easy it is to distort the truth. Often such stories have been generated by the disaffected who have rebelled when legitimate church discipline has been applied to them. As we shall see, the church has not been accustomed to exercising or receiving discipline for some time, and church members do not always take kindly to it even when it is rightly and lovingly exercised. No doubt there is a residue of scare stories that are true, but it is a much, much smaller number than popular rumour would suggest, and probably no more than would be produced about any other group if we looked closely enough.

What is not in doubt, however, is that the whole issue of authority and submission is at the core of many sections of the restoration movement of the present day, and in a way and to a degree that has not been true of previous such movements. The rumour industry is due to the fact that the question of authority has been talked up to a point of great prominence, and that restoration churches have tended to adopt authority models in their structuring of church life, with the result that those who do not agree with these methods tend to look for abuses in order to discredit them. Even those who would disagree however, are bound to acknowledge that the degree of commitment achieved in such churches exceeds that produced by less 'authoritarian' churches. The strength of the movement lies in its ability to mobilize and command the human and financial resources at its disposal. At the beginnings of the movement in the early and mid-seventies 'authority and submission' were presented as key concepts in the restoration of the church. Against dispensational theologies which relegated it to the millennium, and in line with modern biblical scholarship, the kingdom of God became a prominent theme once again. God in Christ had destroyed the rule of Satan and established his own rule through his Son. The essence of the kingdom of God was God's authority and the willingness of his people to let him exercise it over them.

So far so good. The important connection at this point relates to the way in which God manifests his rule, namely through 'delegated authorities' whom he appoints as his agents and through whom his authority is exercised. In the house-church movement, Ephesians 4:11–12 is a key section of the word of God: 'It was he [Christ] who gave some to be apostles, some to be prophets, some to be evangelists, and some to be pastors and teachers, to prepare God's people for works of service, so that the body of Christ may be built up . . .' The ascended Christ carries out his ongoing ministry in the church through delegated authorities whom he has appointed. These are understood as the fivefold ministry of the apostle (responsible for planting churches, laying foundations, overseeing pastors and churches, pioneering the work and the building of the church); the prophet (responsible for perceiving and setting direction); the evangelist (preaching and winning the lost) and the pastor and teacher (caring for the flock on an ongoing basis). How Christians relate to these authorities is crucial if they are to receive what Christ is giving through them and if they are truly to be in the kingdom of God. A kingdom person is one who has submitted his life to a delegated authority and similarly a kingdom church is one which submits to an apostle or a prophet.

In this perception of the kingdom of God we are left with a situation where every person is under the authority (sometimes called the 'covering') of somebody else. Wives and children are under the authority of the husband and father who is God's delegated authority in the home and family. Husbands are under the authority of the elders of the church who, in their turn, are under the authority of apostles and prophets and these men submit to one another. To be truly in the kingdom everyone must submit to another who is over them in the Lord and who can call them to account and help them to mature. Such a person has the right to 'speak into their lives' (to use the cliché) on any matter at all and sometimes (in the case of full-time workers) the one who is subject pays their tithe to the one who is in authority, on the basis of Galatians 6:6. A result of this understanding is that churches are divided into 'kingdom' churches and the rest.

A high value is placed on being in submission to an authority who can be the expression of the kingdom in one's own life. This approach is sometimes called 'shepherding' or 'discipling' and expressions of it have been softened over the years away from an attitude which gives another the right to rule and decide towards one which sees the 'authority' as a helper and a provoker towards greater maturity. Nevertheless, the basic model is that of an authority structure.

This model leads to the development in church life of an authority which is vested in the delegated authorities. Apostles rule and appoint elders in local churches. Elders rule in the local church and are over the people. Democracy therefore is thought to be hostile to the kingdom of God. The kingdom is expressed when the elders are allowed to rule, although if they are wise, they listen carefully to the people.

Clearly, individual churches in the restoration movement have their own expressions of the model just described and it is applied in a variety of styles. Those which stress the concept of delegated authority, however, are at the end of the day refining the one model which sees a network of authority relationships as crucial to the kingdom of God. The question at this point becomes, how does this understanding of the church stand up under the scrutiny of Jesus and the New Testament?

The first thing to be said is that issues of authority and submission are entirely scriptural in essence. When Jesus appointed the seventy he stressed the authority given to them in his name over the powers of evil and towards those to whom they went preaching the good news: 'I have given you authority to trample on snakes and scorpions, and to overcome all the power of the enemy' (Lk 10:19); 'He who listens to you listens to me; he who rejects you rejects me; but he who rejects me rejects him who sent me' (Lk 10:16).

To discuss the nature of the authority given to the church, its members and ministers, is an entirely legitimate issue and it needs to be recognized that every group of Christians has a way of expressing authority and submission even though it may be unacknowledged.

On the other hand, Jesus issued a specific warning precisely at this point in saying, 'The kings of the Gentiles lord it over them; and those who exercise authority over them call themselves Benefactors. *But you are not to be like that*' (Lk 22:25, 26). For Jesus, the church was to be distinguished from the unbelieving world precisely by the way it did and did not practise authority. It is crucially important that authority should be rightly expressed in the church. With this in mind there are various areas in which points may be made concerning current expressions of authority.

Authority and the church—some misunderstandings

The church and the kingdom are not identical

At first this may appear a rather fine distinction, but it is an important one. The kingdom or 'rule' of God is both a present and a future reality. The day is coming when everything in heaven and earth will be subject to God's authority—this is the certain future reality. But in anticipation of this, the kingdom of God is already present among us having been announced by Jesus and having taken root in the lives of men and women willing to yield to it. God's kingdom is his dynamic rule over us. The church is the community of the kingdom, the gathering of those who have received the kingdom of God. It is a sign of the kingdom, bearing witness to the reality of it, and it is an instrument of the kingdom, advancing the rule of God on earth. But it is not itself the kingdom of God. God's kingdom is seen in his immediate and direct rule over us. Once we begin to identify church and kingdom as if they are the same reality, we begin to make static and fixed what is essentially dynamic and free.

No one form or style of church life can claim of itself to be the kingdom of God; if it does it has exalted itself beyond measure. The most it can claim is to serve the kingdom. All church structures must be understood in temporary terms and must be constantly coming under review to see if they still serve the purposes of the kingdom. The kingdom of God is greater than any one church, any one kind of church or the whole of the church. The importance of this distinction is that it keeps the church in a place of relative and not of absolute importance, and reminds us to be modest about the section of the church to which we belong. It also warns us that what serves the kingdom today may fail to do so tomorrow.

The church is not a hierarchy

Traditionally, there have been two ways of understanding the church—from the top down or from the bottom up. Those who have worked from the top down have tended to identify the church with the kingdom and to argue that the true church is to be found where certain ministries are present. The church is thus understood in terms of a hierarchy which gives validity to the local congregation. The most obvious form of this is Roman Catholicism which has identified the kingdom of God with itself and its own structures. Under pressure from schismatic groups, the principle was articulated in the early days that 'the church is where the bishop is'. It is therefore the bishop, his authority and oversight, which make the local church a proper church. The church is understood in terms of its hierarchy. Bishops themselves are valid as they are in the stream of historical continuity which goes back to Peter and the apostles. There may be Christians and congregations which are not related to this historic episcopate; real though their faith may be, they are nevertheless lacking and therefore questionable—they lack full validity.

The house-church movement is far removed from Roman Catholicism but it is interesting to note how parallel some of the thought forms are even though the language may differ. Proceeding from a model of delegated authority which sees Christ delegating his authority to apostles who in turn delegate to pastors and elders, great store is laid upon an 'apostolic foundation', by which is meant not just a deposit of teaching communicated by an apostle, but an ongoing relationship with an apostolic ministry. Churches can therefore be divided into those which have an apostolic foundation and those which do not. Those which do not may be composed of genuine believers but are lacking in this regard and therefore their full validity as genuinely scriptural or kingdom churches is to be questioned.

Apostles are not to be recognized by an historical or institutional process (unlike the historic episcopate), but charismatically and functionally by the quality of their lives and of their workmanship. Consciously or unconsciously behind this latter view there lies a hierarchical understanding of the church. In the early days of the modern restoration movement, this was explicitly articulated in hierarchical terms but recently the tendency has been to withdraw from a pyramid model and to soften it. Nevertheless, the mentality produced by a model can remain even if the explicit model is disowned or qualified at a later time. What is needed to be free of it is a reworking of the basic model and of its implications. There is no doubt that this has been done or is being done by some streams of the restoration movement but until it is done on a thoroughgoing basis some of the fruits of the hierarchical view will remain. These fruits include a tendency to identify a particular way of doing things with the way it should be done; a tendency to deny full recognition to believers and churches who lack the necessary relationships with delegated authorities and to be judgemental towards them; a tendency towards a party mentality, dividing up the church according to which apostle 'covers' which churches, and a tendency towards a consciousness of man and man's approval in the forming of the church which risks obscuring the headship of Christ.

Historically, churches in the radical tradition have sought to work out their doctrine of the church from the bottom up rather than from the top down. The reason for this is not only that they were working from Scripture but that they were in reaction against hierarchical systems of church government which were manifestly corrupt. The passage of Scripture which has been significantly formative in this is Matthew 18:19–20: 'Again, I tell you that if two of you on earth agree about anything you ask for, it will be done for you by my Father in heaven. For where two or three come together in my name, there am I with them.' In Jewish tradition, a synagogue needed a quorum of ten men (not women) in order to function. Here Jesus is saying that the church has authority to function whenever two or three men or women come together in his name. The immediately preceding verses indicate that this authority is of a disciplining and decision-making kind. The point here is not what number should constitute a church but that the presence of Jesus is what confers validity and authority upon a church. In contrast to the hierarchical view which thrusts authority and decision-making up the pyramid, this view thrusts it downward and locates it in the presence of Christ among his people, any of his people. To speak of 'governmental' authority therefore as if this is exclusively in the hands of delegated authorities is to pose a concept of the church at variance with Jesus' words. Government is located in the presence of Christ among his people. This is not to deny that there are ministries which are given to the body, whether they be apostles or elders or others, but it does lead to a radical shift in the way in which such ministries are viewed. To this point we now turn.

Delegated authority is a misleading concept

We have already asserted that Christ appoints ministries and sends them out with his authority. He also asserts that, 'He who receives you receives me, and he who receives me receives the one who sent me. Anyone who receives a prophet because he is a prophet will receive a prophet's reward . . .' (Mt 10:40–41).

The appropriate response to one who is sent by Christ is that we 'receive' them and through them receive what God is giving via them. This is the element of submission that is required of believers. But it needs to be understood that what we are actually receiving is the Lord, and that of the Lord which is being manifested in his ministers.

In saying this we are implying two things. Firstly, what a minister of Christ says and does is not necessarily of the Lord just because he says or does it (most ministers will concede this). A minister may speak the truth, but it is not the truth because he speaks it. It is the authority of *the Lord* through a man which is important and not the authority of the man.

Secondly, this of itself implies the right and responsibility of each of us to discern for ourselves what is of the Lord. That we have the right and capacity to discern is taught by 1 John 2:27: 'As for you, the anointing you received from him remains in you, and you do not need anyone to teach you. But as his anointing teaches you about all things and as that anointing is real, not counterfeit—just as it has taught you, remain in him.' Any teaching or any person which would deprive us of the freedom to discern the mind of God for ourselves cannot be right. Authority rightly exercised in the church of God respects the freedom of those towards whom it is exercised.

This can be expressed in a different way by asserting that Jesus does not delegate his lordship. He is the only Lord in the church and exercises his lordship directly over the life of the individual believer and not through a system of intermediaries. The individual believer is directly accountable to God in his own conscience and not primarily via any other person. The New Testament is careful to attribute headship in the church to Jesus alone. No man can claim to be head of the church, *or of a church,* since Jesus alone is the head.

1 Corinthians 11:3 is significant, 'The head of every man is Christ.' Jesus is directly head of each man and not indirectly

so through 'delegated authorities'. This secular concept of delegation is unhelpful because it fails to safeguard the freedom of the individual and the fact that God is immediately, directly and personally in touch with all who are in the kingdom quite apart from any of the ministries that he has also provided.

In contrast to the current move of restoration which has sought to affirm the lordship of Christ by emphasizing the human authorities which are set in the church, previous movements, Anabaptists and Baptists among them, have sought to magnify the lordship of Christ by de-emphasizing such authorities, by asserting that no man can ever substitute for Jesus in the church. This has led them to develop non-authoritarian structures precisely to make the point clear that the authority belongs to him.

The way the New Testament expresses the authority of the ministries in the church is in terms of 'sending'. Christ sends ministers and they have authority in so far as they fulfil the mission on which they have been sent. This commission simultaneously affirms their authority in the exercise of their mission and denies it in spheres outside their mission. The authority is the authority of the message rather than of the messenger.

Practically, this means that a minister of God may apply and affirm with authority that which is clearly set out in God's word but he must make much room for freedom before God in those things which are not clearly so. This is not to imply that at these points his counsel is no better than anybody else's. It ought to carry great weight and will do so if it is good counsel. But it cannot be enforced as if it had equal authority with the word of God. In all these things he exercises towards God's people an enabling and serving ministry focused on Christ and not a dominating rulership focused on himself. Paul expressed it in this way, 'I promised you to one husband, to Christ, so that I might present you as a pure virgin to him' (2 Cor 11:2).

Jesus our model for authority and leadership

We have sought to indicate at different points that, whereas all the Scriptures have authority, not all points of Scripture are normative for us. Although we learn from the Old Testament, we do not make it normative for our behaviour since it has been fulfilled and surpassed in Christ. This is true of our understanding of authority as of many other themes. For instance, Exodus 18, a passage frequently used to advocate the concept and practice of delegated authority, cannot simply be taken out of the Old Testament and used as a model for the structure of the church today without explaining, by reference to Christ, the criterion by which a section of the Old Testament is made normative for those who are in the new covenant.

Likewise, David cannot be taken as the example of what the government of the church ought to be like today without some theological justification, by reference to Christ, of how David can become normative over against Jesus. If we follow David too closely at this point we end up with a church in which the authority model is a military one—and this is precisely what some churches have argued for and achieved. The elders are equated with the officers, the members with the rank and file. The inadequacy of these models is their failure to make Jesus the norm for the nature and practice of authority in the church.

As we have seen from Luke 22:25–26, Jesus explicitly taught his disciples that they were to be radically different from the nations precisely in the area of authority. The heart of the difference consists in not 'lording it' over people, that is in not dominating them in a way that deprives them of freedom. Authority is not to be coercive but is to be the authority of a servant.

In Luke 22:26 Jesus immediately tells his disciples how they are to be different from the nations: 'The greatest among you should be like the youngest, and the one who rules like the one who serves.' For this the disciples have

Jesus' own example, 'I am among you as one who serves' (v.27). Servant authority is exercised by example and by the winning of people to a voluntary obedience born of love. In his life, Jesus demonstrated this by leading his disciples patiently and gently, setting before them an example of how they also should walk. He did not indoctrinate them in the faith but drew it out of their developing understanding of who he was. He put up with their squabbles and failings, and from time to time rebuked them sharply, but he did not dominate them or devalue their own freedom of mind or of action. This is the style of leadership which is binding for all who operate in his name.

Servant authority is more than benevolence. A benevolent dictator is still a dictator. Servant authority is not just a style of leadership but a category of leadership. It refuses to compromise the freedom of those who are served by it. When it has to do with sin and evil, it will be, as Jesus was, direct and uncompromising in its attitude, but in all other circumstances it will seek to persuade people by the power of example and by the wooing influence of love towards a better way.

Over recent years a new emphasis has been placed on the importance of leaders and leadership. Where leadership is understood according to the Jesus model this is well and good, but it is important to remember the warnings Jesus gave about elitism. In Matthew 23:8–12 he says: 'But you are not to be called "Rabbi" for you have only one Master and you are all brothers. And do not call anyone on earth "father", for you have one Father, and he is in heaven. Nor are you to be called "teacher", for you have one Teacher, the Christ. The greatest among you will be your servant. For whoever exalts himself will be humbled, and whoever humbles himself will be exalted.' The concern of Jesus here is that among his disciples (in contrast to the Pharisees) the exercise of leadership authority should neither obscure the supremacy of God and of his Christ nor the fact that the church is a brotherhood before it is a hierarchy. The effect of this is to de-emphasize leadership rather than the reverse. Jesus issued his warning because the temptation to exalt leaders and put them in place of God is always with us. It is with us because of the human tendency to refuse to take personal responsibility for ourselves and for situations and to want others to do this for us. It is with us because of the equally strong inclination we have to bask in the reflected glory of a competent and admired leader and to imagine that because we are connected with them we may somehow attribute their qualities to ourselves. The restoration emphasis on leadership has much to commend it but in the light of Jesus' words it has as many dangers as it has possibilities.

Before moving on, let us consider what *is* the place of hierarchy in the church. Experience and Scripture indicate that no group, Christian or otherwise, can function adequately without formalizing a hierarchical structure of some kind, however low key it may be. The important distinction to make is that between an economic hierarchy and an essential hierarchy. An economic hierarchy is a leadership structure which emerges within a group for the fulfilling of the group's purpose. As such the hierarchy is a group function, drawing its authority from the group and remaining accountable to it and within it. An essential hierarchy is understood as being of the essence of the group (the church is where the bishop is) and as giving validity to it. This distinction corresponds to that already made between constructing a doctrine of the church from the 'top down' (essential) or from the 'bottom up' (economic); the thrust of the argument presented throughout this chapter is towards seeing whatever hierarchies are established in the church as 'economic', functional and non-sacrosanct.

The government of the church

One of the anomalies that can be discerned in the restoration branches of the charismatic movement is that whereas emphasis has increasingly been laid on the participation of the whole of the body of Christ in worship and ministry, participation of the whole body in the government of the church has been denied. The priesthood of all believers is to be worked out in the worship of the church by the operation of spiritual gifts and in ministries, but decision-making is seen as an activity which is to be restricted to the wise and the anointed, to those 'governmental' authorities which are set in the church for this purpose. In this willingness to submit to a governmental authority, the ordinary church member is receiving the kingdom of God as it is expressed through a delegated authority. 'Democracy', government of the people by the people for the people, is seen as being one of the great evils of the church and opposed to the kingdom of God. In contrast to this, God is now restoring a true governmental understanding and structure in the church. Democracy (rule by the people) is not theocracy (rule by God), we are told, but oligarchy (rule by a few) apparently is.

The flaw in the argument presented here is revealed by the fact that the kingdom of God cannot be identified with any one human model of government. To substitute for a democratic model of church life one which places government in the hands of a few and reserves decision-making to them is no more of necessity a 'kingdom' model than any other. It is equally likely to be misused and misled, even more so if it is proclaimed to be the kingdom model which eclipses all others. The fact is that the kingdom of God cannot be reduced to a system or a method of government; to concentrate power in the hands of a few people is a dangerous and non-Christian thing to do, since power corrupts.

Traditionally there have been three models of church government: the episcopal, the presbyterian and the congregational. Episcopal government, such as is practised in the Catholic and Anglican churches, operates with a hierarchical view of the church focusing authority in the bishop who represents Christ's authority. Presbyterian government locates authority in a presbytery of elders who together direct and decide. Congregational government sees the involvement of the whole congregation in the decision-making process as essential, understanding the church in non-hierarchical terms and witnessing to this by making the church meeting the final human authority in a local church under God.

In practice most forms of government are a balancing of forces and to all intents and purposes episcopal, presbyterian and congregational forms may look very similar and function alike. This is equally true of the restoration church. People may not have a constitutional vote but they can still at the end of the day vote with their feet, so however much authority is given to elders they still have to listen to the people in order to lead effectively.

Ultimately the church of God is not a democracy or an oligarchy. It is a distinct form of government which Karl Barth described as 'a brotherly Christocracy'. Jesus, and he alone, is the head of the church and his will is discerned among the brethren. For all of us involved in the government of the church the essential question is, What does Jesus want and how do we find that out?

Jesus is not restricted to any one form of church government. Sometimes he may choose to speak through an episcopal figure (whether bishop or apostle), sometimes through a group of leaders (such as elders) and sometimes through the people (on the congregational model).

The book of Acts yields evidence for each of these approaches. Peter asked no man's permission when he rebuked Ananias and Sapphira (Acts 5:1–11) but acted on his own authority. On the other hand, when it came to the appointment of the seven (Acts 6) the appointments were handed over to the church for decision. In the case of the appointment of Saul and Barnabas to the missionary task (Acts 13) it was to the leading elders that the Holy Spirit spoke, and they acted on the strength of his word. In Acts 15 we see a fine balance of forces at the Council of Jerusalem. As the issue of circumcising the Gentiles was discussed, Peter, Barnabas and

Paul had a major voice in the deliberations as apostolic figures, James summed up and articulated the (episcopal) consensus (vv. 13–21), yet the context was that of an apostles' and elders' (presbyterian) conference (v. 4) and verse 22 says, 'Then the apostles and elders, *with the whole church,* decided to choose some of their own men . . .' (congregational).

The point is that no one approach to church government is adequate because Christ is greater than any human authority. The will of Christ for his church may be communicated for seasons of time or over specific issues through one person, through a group of persons or through the whole church. Our task is to hear the voice of the Lord wherever it may be coming from at any given time. To identify the kingdom of God with any one structure of church life is to misunderstand the nature of the kingdom as God's dynamic rule over his church—a rule which cannot be tied down to static forms. Rather than assert the priority of one form of church government we do well to express the New Testament vision in the form of three values.

The headship of Christ

Jesus Christ is the Head of the church and the church exists by him and for him (Col 1:15–20). The church belongs to no man and no man can claim 'headship' within Christ's body. The church is not a democracy where the will of the majority prevails, it is a community where Christ rules and reigns. His will is paramount. The church is not intended to be a battleground for competing human interests, neither does it fit any of the standard human systems of government, whether they be autocracy (rule by one man), oligarchy (rule by a few) or democracy (rule by the people). It is Christ's church and the only thing that counts is knowing and doing his will as disclosed in Scripture and as witnessed to by the Holy Spirit in the church. This is why the church exists and why submission to the Head is required in all things.

Leadership

It should not be assumed from the previous point that leaders are unnecessary in the church. Christ the Head has specifically appointed leaders in his body in order that the church may function. Their task is to give leadership and they are to be honoured, received and submitted to in that capacity. Their leadership is exercised by teaching and example (1 Pet 5:1–4) and is a service for the people and not a dominance over people (Mt 20:25–28). Scripture is clear that we are to conceive of the church primarily as a brotherhood, or a family, rather than as a hierarchy (Mt 23:8–12) but we are to honour the leadership task highly (Heb 13:17).

Consensus

It cannot be assumed that leaders have a monopoly on discernment. Not all believers are leaders but all believers are priests and therefore have access to the mind and heart of God (1 Pet 2:9). The will of God is paramount in the church, but how is it to be discerned? To affirm consensus means that all God's people have a role in the discernment process. This is not to say that all opinions are of equal value but it does mean that the Holy Spirit does not speak exclusively through leaders. He can speak through anybody who is a member of his body (1 Jn 2:20, 26–27). Therefore the church moves and grows as it perceives God's mind together.

These values are more important than which structures we happen to operate with. They are capable of being expressed within a variety of formal structures whether episcopal, presbyterian or congregational. At the end of the day what matters is that the church discerns and does the will of God. Where it is the heart of the people to do this (and that is the crucial issue) the authority question resolves itself without the need to resort to authoritarian and powerful structures. Jesus Christ is the authority in the church and through his spiritual presence that authority can be made known.

Power and authority

There is a difference between authority and power. This distinction is most vividly illustrated in the life of Jesus, who, though a man of immense authority, was powerless in human terms. Power brings the ability to command, to enforce one's will; authority brings the ability to win people's willing obedience without resorting to power. The enemies of Jesus, the Pharisees, the Sadducees and the Romans, had all the power but none of the authority.

When followers of Jesus seek to build power structures in the name of the church or the kingdom they are in danger of departing from the way of powerlessness exemplified by Jesus himself. The dictum that power corrupts, although not biblical in origin, is as true of the church as it is of the world. The authority of Jesus was derived from the quality of his person, his anointing with the Holy Spirit and the dedication of his love for us demonstrated in the cross. This is the pathway of powerless authority which has been shown to be God's way through the incarnation.

When, as has been done recently, we seek to understand Christian relationships in terms of power or command structures, we risk distorting them. Prominence has been given to the concept of a 'chain of command' in marriage, for instance. Out of a concern to stress who is 'in charge' in the husband-wife relationship, the hierarchical model, which sees a chain of command from God to husband to wife, has been widely employed in restoration circles. Yet in a loving relationship the issue of 'chains of command' fades to a point of insignificance. Marriage is not primarily a hierarchical, military-style relationship in which commands are given, but a loving partnership of a man and a woman in Christ in which neither dominates but both seek to please the other. To reduce such a relationship to a chain of command is to miss the point of marriage, and when Paul deals with this subject in his letters his concern is not to demonstrate the chain of command but the way of love. This is the true context for 'submission'. We are to submit not because we live in a hierarchy which requires it but because we follow a Saviour who has taught us how to live in self-denying, self-giving love.

What is true of marriage is true of the church. The church is a love structure before it is a power structure. Authority grows out of love not love out of the acceptance of authority. To give prominence to 'delegated authority' and command structures distorts the nature of the church as a loving, open, accepting, serving community in which, like Jesus, we renounce the use of power and coercion in favour of self-giving. But in such renunciation, far from 'losing out' on the manifestation of authority we actually establish the base on which authority—Jesus-like authority—can be known among us through the presence of Christ in our midst. We decrease in order that his presence among us may increase. It is in this way, not through the establishing of human power structures, that the kingdom of God will be expressed through his people.

6

Restoration and Church Discipline

Discipleship: authority, submission and the kingship model

Whatever we may make of current attempts to understand the nature of authority and submission in the life of the church, and however much we may want to qualify and correct these, it is necessary to recognize the concern out of which the re-emphasis on authority has emerged. It is the desire to rediscover discipleship, namely a serious and rigorous following after Jesus, that is at the root of these concerns, and the apparent failure of many forms of church life to produce disciples has led some members of the body to search for forms and practices which will. In the early church being a Christian and being a disciple were synonymous, indeed believers were known as disciples before they were called Christians. It was at Antioch that the disciples were first called Christians (Acts 11:26).

In much of the church today discipleship is seen as an option which Christians are exhorted to choose if they want to. Apparently there are those who are content to be Christians without the cost of being disciples. It is in reaction to this that prominence has been given to the nature of the church as a discipling community which is not content to allow the congregation simply to congregate but which is seeking to form and fashion its members into followers of Jesus. This presupposes on the part of the church members a willingness to submit to authority which is the precision tool with which their lives can be corrected and changed.

Some biblical justification is given to this school of thought by reference to *the institution of kingship* in ancient Israel. At the end of the period of the judges, an era of charismatic and sporadic leadership, the statement is made: 'In those days Israel had no king; *everyone did as he saw fit*' (Judg 21:25). The RSV translates this: 'Every man did what was right in his own eyes.' This is interpreted to indicate a lack of cohesion and direction among the people of God. Individualism and anarchy were the order of the day, with no sense of government. The people were like sheep without a shepherd. This may be likened to the condition of the contemporary church which is also riddled with anarchy and the wrong kind of independence. Not only the church but specifically the charismatic movement may be likened to the people under the judges. Charismatic experience there may be, but anarchy and disorder exist alongside it and call its value into question.

In this way the scene is set both in ancient Israel and in the contemporary church, specifically in its charismatic expressions, for a new experience of authority. In ancient Israel a kingship is established which, notwithstanding its false start in Saul (another 'charismatic' lacking the right qualities), finds glorious and triumphant expression in David, who rules over the people and brings them into an age of unrivalled prosperity. David understands the nature of delegated authority and rules over the people through precisely such a system of government. In a parallel way, we are told, what is needed to deliver the church from anarchy—even in the charismatic renewal—is a new experience of governmental authority giving direction, cohesion and security and delivering the people from doing what is right 'in their own eyes'. God is restoring his kingdom, and the government of the church through his delegated authorities is again being experienced. This recovery heralds for us a new age in the life of the church, possibly even a golden age as was experienced under David. Again the opportunity is taken to point out the difference between churches and kingdom churches. The latter are those which are under a delegated authority, the former are living in the spiritual equivalent of the era of the judges.

This particular way of understanding the institution of kingship in Israel picks up the favourable light in which the Davidic era is portrayed in Scripture. He is one of the major figures of the Old Testament. Under his rule the fortunes of Israel are at their highest point, their enemies are defeated, their borders are extended, Jerusalem becomes the seat of government and plans are made for the building of the temple. Moreover, David is the forerunner of the Christ who is to be born of his line and is to sit on his throne.

However, in other portions of Scripture, the concept and practice of kingship, although significant, is heavily criticized and is presented not as God's will and intention but as an accommodation to the wilfulness of the people.

To understand this we need to do justice to 1 Samuel 8 where the people are described as approaching Samuel, their last judge, to ask for a king to be appointed to rule over them. Samuel is told by God to give them what they ask for, but the passage makes abundantly clear that this is a concession by God to them and not an expression of his will. There are three specific cricitisms of kingship which emerge.

To ask for a king to rule over them is *a rejection of the kingship of God*. 'And the Lord told him: "Listen to all that the people are saying to you; it is not you they have rejected as their king, but me"' (v.7). Far from being a positive action, the request for a king is a symptom of the age-old struggle of man against God. To let God be King is too costly an undertaking for men to engage in since it means dealing with God directly. The request for a ruler is an evasion of confrontation with God himself.

To ask for a king to rule over them is *a choice to be 'like the nations'*. 'We want a king over us. Then we shall be like all the other nations, with a king to lead us and to go out before us and fight our battles' (vv.19–20). For a nation which was called to be different from all the other nations this represented a sad failure of understanding and of faith. Apparently it was too difficult to trust God to fight their battles for them as he had promised to do. For Israel, security was to be found in imitating the nations, not in trusting God. Here again, kingship represents failure to rise to the vocation God intended for Israel. It stands for compromise and conformity with the world.

To ask for a king to rule over them *opens up the way for new forms of exploitation*. 'Now listen to them; but warn them solemnly and let them know what the king who will reign over them will do' (v.9). Samuel's warning is that power corrupts. He tells them in a sixfold repetition that a king will take from them and not give to them. The result of this will be that 'you will cry out for relief from the king you have chosen' (v.18). To adopt worldly power structures is to invite worldly consequences.

If we are being invited to see a parallel between the institution of kingship and the restoration of 'government' to the church, honesty compels us to do justice to the inner critique of kingship given in this chapter. To opt for these new governmental structures in the church carries with it the same dangers and risks as did the institution of kingship. We need to be careful that in setting up men as authorities and powerful figures we are not thereby actually rejecting God who desires to rule directly over his people; we need to be careful that we are not imitating the world in its desire for 'heroes' and 'leaders' who will fight our battles for us; we need to be careful that we are not opening the door to forces which will rob us of our freedom and seek to exploit us. God accommodated himself to the idea of kingship and took it into his plan, but it is clear that it was not the full expression of his will and we should not take anything other than the full expression of his will as our norm in the church. At this point, as at all others, we must be led back to Jesus who is the exact representation of God's being as our model and norm for issues of discipline and discipling.

Discipling: the three dimensions

The point of our discussion so far is that one option in the making of disciples is to develop authoritarian structures, but that this is an option to be avoided. We need to move beyond this towards a positive statement of how the church may function as a discipling community without resorting to authoritarian methods. We shall do this by reviewing three dimensions of the discipling process before attempting to understand the nature of discipline in the Christian community.

In the previous chapter we touched on three classical forms of church government. Episcopacy stresses the individual government or oversight of the church by a bishop, Presbyterianism locates the government of the church in a group of elders and congregationalism finds it among the people in the corporate mind of the church. These forms of church order correspond to three dimensions in the discipling process and represent a tendency to lay a stress on one or other of them. These dimensions are the personal, the collegial and the corporate.

The personal

In this dimension stress is laid upon the role played by specific individuals in governing, overseeing and discipling the church. Certain individuals are called and appointed by God to function in this area. The apostle exercises this function on a translocal basis. The more traditional form of the personal stresses the place of the bishop as the overseer of the churches. The papacy is one form of personal oversight, placing the whole of the church as it does under one man.

In other circles, emphasis is placed upon the need for each believer to be personally accountable to one man. This trend has been known in recent years as the 'shepherding' or 'discipling' movement and has argued that each man should oversee his family and should himself be overseen by a personal shepherd who attempts to disciple him in the ways of the Lord. Biblical justification is given to this by reference to the practice of Jesus in gathering twelve disciples around him. Jesus taught the multitudes but discipled only twelve men whom he personally instructed, shaped, rebuked and mobilized as he shared his life with them. Jesus commanded his disciples to go and make disciples and this is understood as the personal shepherding of a number of men as he himself had done.

When this model of personal oversight is adopted in the church there are two clear benefits. 1) It provides a structure for supervising closely the life of the whole church and of each individual within it. Difficulties, aberrations and needs should therefore be easily and swiftly detected. 2) It provides a precision tool whereby an individual may be confronted with the need to mature as a disciple and helped towards that end.

Accordingly, some restoration churches have developed shepherding/discipling structures in which every member is receiving such personal oversight. This extends through to the pastors who are being themselves pastored, sometimes by men in different continents!

In popular usage it was the custom to call this practice 'covering', although this is now on the wane, probably because of the extremely slender biblical basis for the term to be used in this way. The word 'covering' is not without its practical uses and there should be no objection to talking about a pastor 'covering' an individual or a situation in the same way that a doctor might 'cover' a case or a patient, but in the shepherding movement the word has assumed a semi-technical significance with overtones of authority and submission. In this sense the word is hard to justify biblically and is falling out of favour.

The place of personal oversight as one of the dimensions of discipling is without question. It is clearly there in Scripture and is of obvious value. Some people are marked out by God for their personal contribution to the life of the church. The question is not whether the personal dimension has a place but to what degree it does and how far it should determine our models of church life. The focus on the personal dimension in the oversight of the church labours under certain difficulties.

1) There is little evidence that the New Testament church was structured in the way advocated by the one-to-one discipling method. References to any system of discipline such as this are notable by their absence. The texts which are appealed to in order to prove the contrary are overloaded to the point where they sink without trace.

2) It is crucial to understand how Jesus is our model in these things. Granted that he discipled twelve men and that he commanded us to go and make disciples, it is fatal to assume that we can disciple in the same way that Jesus did. Jesus made disciples of himself and we are called to make disciples of Jesus and not of ourselves. True discipling is teaching men to follow Jesus, not other men. Granted, Paul was able to say, 'Follow my example, as I follow the example of Christ' (1 Cor 11:1). We can all serve from time to time as partial reflections of Jesus—worthy of imitation in some things, where we closely follow him, but partial reflections is the most that we are. Jesus is the discipler; we are not. To overestimate our ability in this area is to exalt ourselves unduly.

3) The evidence of the New Testament is that the apostles and elders of the early church did not so much oversee individual lives as churches. Individual lives were overseen as they related to and affected the church, but not in isolation or distinction from it.

These points do not eliminate the need for the personal dimension of oversight in the church, but they do relativize it. A church that is constructed on a personal model is not one that can look wholeheartedly to the New Testament for support. Personal discipling is one aspect of the total discipling process. It is a precision tool to be used from time to time as necessity requires. There will be times and seasons and situations when believers, especially believers in leadership, will need specific and personal discipling to enable them to follow Christ more faithfully, to tease through a difficulty, to negotiate a course or to confront a problem. Yet the personal dimension remains but one weapon in the armoury and when it is used should be used with the specific understanding that no one can deprive a child of God of their responsibility before God whose rule over his children is direct.

From another tradition there comes an example of personal oversight which is capable of wide application throughout the church and which need not conflict with the cautionary remarks already made. In the Catholic tradition stress has been laid upon the place of a spiritual director, namely a trusted and respected fellow believer to whom confession can be made and from whom counsel and direction may be received. For those anxious to make spiritual progress the discipline of submission to a spiritual director who exists as an enabler and encourager of spiritual growth is a valuable tool. This is particularly true of that anomalous breed, the unpastored pastor. If there is a case to be made anywhere for continuing and regular personal oversight it is for those whose continual task is the feeding and nurturing of the flock of God. The character of those who minister is as important in their work as any other aspect of their training and since pastors are also in a continual process of formation here is an important point at which the precision tool of personal oversight needs consistent use. Pastors function best when they are personally encouraged and excited and it is vital to discover forms of oversight which can sustain this attitude of heart and mind.

The collegial

This dimension of pastoral oversight and discipline stresses the need for a 'college' or team of persons to be working together in a complementary fashion for the wellbeing of the Christian community. As we have seen, the New Testament indicates the personal dimension of oversight and discipling but this is never seen in an extremely individualist sense. Personal ministries are exercised from within the security of a team of workers who are supporting and complementing one another. We see this operating in the ministry of Jesus when he gathers a team of twelve men with differing but complementary personalities and gifts. We see it in Acts when the apostles function together in the establishing of the church. We see it in the church at Antioch when the Holy Spirit speaks to the gathering of elders concerning Saul and Barnabas. We see it in the ministry of Paul and Barnabas who operate with a team of workers in the apostolic ministry and who appoint elders in the churches they plant. The pattern of New Testament church life indicates a plurality of leaders or of ministries in the church.

The benefits of this are relatively obvious. Plurality facilitates mutual support, mutual correction, shared wisdom and complementarity. The security afforded in this way to a leadership team ought to be reflected by greater security in the church. Equally, the accountability that collegiality affords ought to cut down the likelihood of mistakes of judgement being made. The principle of plurality also sheds further light on the personal dimension of the discipling process. Personal ministries are exercised from within the security of a collegial base, enhancing that base and increasing its effectiveness. There is no New Testament warrant for the highly individualistic and personalized ministries which are found in some sectors of today's church and which operate without being accountable to such a base.

The rediscovery of plural forms of spiritual oversight is a marked feature of the contemporary church and is radically altering the face of local church life across the board as churches of different backgrounds find ways of recognizing and appointing such teams.

The corporate

This dimension of oversight highlights the involvement of the whole church in the task of discipling one another. The care and wellbeing of the church cannot be confined to the personal and collegial dimensions. We are all involved and we are all responsible. Moreover, since Christ is the one who disciples his people, the discipling task is not the task of any individual but of the whole community since only the fullness of the body can actualize the fullness of Christ. The body is the agency whereby we learn of Christ and are called to imitate him as he is revealed to us in the differing members of that body. Ultimately, therefore, the nurturing, oversight and discipling of Christians is the responsibility of the whole church.

If there is a model of the church which predominates in the New Testament it is the corporate model, and the collegial and personal dimensions of oversight need to be seen as functions and expressions of the corporate responsibility of the body to care for its members and to lead them into the ways of Christ. To affirm this is of great importance because once again it locates authority and responsibility in the church and not in a hierarchy.

Which model is primary?

The personal, collegial and corporate dimensions of oversight are all important, but where we place the emphasis determines what shape of church we end up with. In the restoration movement different streams place the emphasis on different dimensions and end up with a different model of the church. Some emphasize the personal and evolve a model based on the one-to-one shepherding of the whole church. Inevitably the end result is pyramid shaped. Others stress the collegial and locate governmental authority very much in the local church eldership. Others stress the corporate and end up with an eldership which operates by the consent and agreement of the people in achieving commonly agreed aims and goals.

It is the twofold contention of this chapter that in the light of the New Testament the corporate model must be primary and it must draw upon the collegial and personal dimensions of oversight and discipling which are designed to enable this function to be fulfilled in and through the whole body of the church.

To substantiate this point Matthew 18:15–20 must be the focus of our investigations and will provide the springboard for the remainder of this chapter.

The stress in these verses is upon the competence of the gathered church. When the church gathers and Jesus is in the midst and when the church finds itself in agreement, then it has authority to decide and to act in the assurance that God will back it up: 'I tell you the truth, whatever you bind on earth will be bound in heaven, and whatever you loose on earth will be loosed in heaven' (v.18).

Something more than the natural authority of a social organization or than self-government is envisaged here. The point is that the church can become an instrument of the authority of its Lord when it is acting in his name and under his rule. We are not talking here of a delegated authority but of the direct exercise of the authority of Christ in the congregation. The decisive point is that Jesus is in the midst. In these circumstances the church's action is the action of God's presence as the church is united with God in Christ.

In the procedure which Jesus outlines for the restoration of the wrongdoer after personal attempts to 'win the brother' have failed and after collegial attempts likewise come to nothing, the ultimate step that can be taken is that which is taken corporately by the church acting in Christ's name. The order is significant. It is when all resources have been exhausted that the church acts. The final appeal is not to a man or men but to the whole church. The highest authority is Christ in the midst of his gathered people.

Let us review the ground we have covered so far. We have seen that the renewed emphasis on authority in the church derives from a desire to recover the proper New Testament stress on discipleship and discipline. The recovery of this emphasis is healthy but is not to be pursued, as some are pursuing it, by a heightened emphasis on governmental authority by analogy with kingship. To do this is to miss the criticisms of kingship offered by the Old Testament itself. The primary model of the church in the New Testament is the corporate model and a recovery of true discipline in the church must be effected along this line, emphasizing the involvement of the whole church in the task of discipling and discipline. The personal and collegial elements of discipling are to be seen as ministries enabling the whole church to function in this way. With this point established we may now consider how this is to be achieved.

Church discipline

The Anabaptists argued that one of the marks of the true church was that it practised church discipline. One of the features of the early English Baptists was that their church meetings (which followed immediately upon their worship meetings) were almost exclusively devoted to disciplinary matters, as their minute books bear testimony. This is what they understood by the 'government' of the church. In this they were following directly the example of the early church which was a powerless community in the worldly sense but which possessed the spiritual authority to excommunicate from its fellowship those who sinned and refused to repent.

Paul gives directions to this effect in 1 Corinthians 5:4, 'When you are assembled in the name of our Lord Jesus and I am with you in spirit, and the power of our Lord Jesus is present, hand this man over to Satan [that is, exclude him from the community of faith], so that the sinful nature may be destroyed and his spirit saved on the day of the Lord.'

Over against this New Testament picture must be placed the unwillingness of the contemporary church to discipline its members. It is at this point that restoration and reformation are necessary in the church as this element is taken with greater seriousness than has been the case. The basis for church discipline may be outlined as follows.

The local church is a discipling community of disciples

To follow after Jesus is to be a disciple. When we submit to him we submit to his yoke and his direction.

In New Testament terms there is no such thing as a believer who is not also a disciple. Discipleship has to do with an active and continuous process of learning from Jesus and living in obedience to him. It is a costly process. In its mission the church preaches the necessity of the obedience of faith. Men and women are called to leave off from their rebellion and obey Christ. Baptism is a sign of this willingness to take up the cross of self-denial. In its ministry, the church wins its members to better discipleship by example, by encouragement and exhortation and, where necessary, by admonishing those of its fellowship who seek to avoid the challenge of discipleship at specific points. All these activities are carried out lovingly and compassionately, not in the spirit of judgement and condemnation but in that of grace and truth.

In the local church all are being discipled and are discipling

As Jesus is the Discipler and is present in all of his body, all believers are involved in the process of discipling as members of that body. The qualities of the Lord which are seen in each of us are worthy of emulation by the rest. The keynote in the local church is mutual submission, the willingness to yield to one another and to the Lord in each other. This implies willingness to receive from each other and to take responsibility for each other. When my brother or sister is falling short it is my responsibility to win them to better things, but to do so gently and humbly. Equally, when I fall short it is my responsibility to receive the correction of my fellow disciples and to do so joyfully.

Discipline is part of the process of discipling

The church has authority to discipline in Jesus' name, that is to act with authority in the case of those who refuse to hear the admonition of their brothers and sisters. This is referred to in Matthew 18:18 as 'binding and loosing' and is an authority which comes from the presence of Christ among his people when they act in accordance with his character and purpose. Thc wording of Paul in 1 Corinthians 5:4 is significant, 'When . . . the power of our Lord Jesus is present' the church is able to act decisively. This surely refers to an experience of the presence and guidance of the Lord on such an occasion.

In the church, discipline is the discipline of integrity. It is not the church enforcing its party line or lording it over the freedom of conscience of its members. To do this is to deviate into the false and oppressive religious authority of the Inquisition and of numerous sects.

True discipline is an extension of the discipling process whereby a believer is encouraged to face up to their conscience and to the demands of the Lord clearly outlined in his word. Where an individual wilfully refuses to do this and persists in disobedience or immorality to the point that it becomes necessary to exclude them from the community of faith, it is being shown to them that they cannot with integrity both claim to be disciples and be wilfully disobedient. Such action, when entered into, is not that of a judgemental band of bigots, but of a people whose desire is to walk in the light. Happily few members of the body prove to be so unwilling to listen to reproof that exclusion becomes necessary.

It must never be lost sight of that the aim of such discipline is to make people face up to their sin and depart from it. Discipline is always intended to be redemptive, not punitive.

It is exercised in compassion and mercy as well as integrity. Discipline has been aptly described as 'gentleness in action'.

Over the years, churches in the radical tradition of the believers' church have sought to take discipline seriously. They have also adopted differing approaches to the issue of 'shunning', that is to the treatment of those who have departed the faith by those who are still in it. Jesus said that such persons are to be treated as pagans or tax collectors (Mt 18:17) and frequently Paul advocates a policy of avoidance of those who are grossly dishonouring the way of Christ (Rom 16:17; 1 Cor 5:11; 2 Thess 3:6, 14; 2 Tim 3:2–5; Tit 3:10). In some groups, avoidance has been carried to such cruel extremes as to bring dishonour upon the very process of discipline. It is best to understand the intention of these verses in terms of fellowship. When a person has blatantly disowned discipleship, Christians should avoid any form of association with that person which would lead them to conclude that their disobedience is being approved of or colluded in. Again, the issue is that of integrity and the quality of our witness, but it is certainly possible to maintain these while offering the normal human courtesies and considerations to backslidden persons. Indeed, this is more likely to win them back than any other policy.

In the restoration of the church of Jesus Christ, it is vital for the church to be renewed in its role as the discipling community. It is also vital to rediscover the ways in which this discipleship was nurtured and encouraged, and the ways in which rejection of discipleship was confronted and challenged, by the believing community both in the New Testament and in church history.

This chapter has attempted to chart a course away from the developing of powerful human structures and systems to effect discipleship towards one which gives full weight to the whole of the church as the human agency whereby discipleship is encouraged and inspired in God's people. It has also attempted to give a perspective which indicates that it is not the human agency as such but the presence of Christ in and among his people which is the crucial element in both discipling and discipline. We have stressed the headship of Christ and his living presence by his Spirit in the body as that which is of supreme importance. Only when these realities are kept clearly in focus will we do justice to the New Testament understanding of the church.

7
Restoration and Contemporary Society

Questioning the radicals

So far in this book we have addressed issues which have been widely discussed over recent years and which therefore have a kind of 'security' attached to them. Familiarity has given them a certain respectability and because the battle lines have been drawn quite precisely over each issue, should any of us begin to feel insecure with our own position we can always retire to the safety of our side's foxholes. We can reasonably assume that in the church we belong to there is an accepted group attitude that will protect us from making ourselves too vulnerable. With this chapter we depart from such security, for in it we raise issues which are likely to cause disagreement in most congregations whatever our attitude may be to charismatic renewal, authority, apostles or shepherding. Because this is so, we tend to avoid discussion of them. 'Radical' churches which have boldly proclaimed to others the need for decision and action about the issues already outlined in this book suddenly become very coy about 'radical' issues over which their own churches are not united. This is because within this very lack of unanimity is the potential for division.

It is interesting to reflect upon the function that self-image has in the life of the church. Once, the radical image did not suit most Christians. They chose to see themselves as conservative guardians of the faith once delivered. Many still do and draw great personal comfort from this image of themselves as bastions of the old gospel in an age of apostasy. The appeal to these conservative instincts has great power in the life of the church and is played upon by many. The fact is that this self-image makes some people feel good, and they adopt such positions not (as they suppose) out of fidelity to Christ but out of deference to their own self-image.

The same applies to radicalism. Once an individual has made the mental shift (as over recent years many have) towards the exciting vision of themselves as pioneering radicals, the urge to be radical can end up as a form of self-indulgence which concludes that 'if it is radical it must be right'. We need to remind ourselves that faithfulness to Jesus is everything and that there is no virtue in conservatism or radicalism in its own right.

Having said that, this chapter poses the question, How radical is radical? The radicalism of the restoration movement of recent years has been directed largely towards the structures of the church. The issues under discussion have focused on the nature of church life and the shape of the Christian community. How is it to be organized, governed and structured? These questions have already been discussed in this book as being of importance, but there is a characteristic danger which besets those who think in this way. We all want to be associated with something that looks good, or at least with something that we can tell ourselves is better than what others have, and this desire is rooted in our flesh. For some this perfectionism, which again feeds on our self-image, can be more important than being effective or useful. It is actually a form of self-righteousness closely linked with Pharisaism. It proclaims that we are the 'kosher' ones and others are not or if they are, not as much as we are. An understanding of 'restoration' which limits its horizons to the church can be a snare indeed. So it is that people who make very radical sounds about the church can simultaneously be arch-conservatives in their attitude to society.

My argument is that if the principles of restoration are faithfully adhered to they will cause us to take a radical stance over against the structures of our society, and that if there is a price to be paid in being radical it is at this point. If we take the New Testament seriously we are compelled to recognize that the church, even the radical church, has hugely accommodated itself to the form of this world in her social attitudes. In fact the average Christian differs little at all from any other citizen.

The church, 'the powers' and the world

In chapter four an analysis of the 'principalities and powers' was outlined which was then applied to the structures of the church. The fallenness of the created order, it was argued, does not solely consist of the souls of men and women but includes the powers, the 'basic principles of the world' of Galatians 4:3, which held us in captivity until we were liberated by Jesus through his cross and resurrection (Col 2:15). These basic principles of human life were further defined as religious, intellectual, moral and political structures. A contemporary sociological analysis would speak purely in these terms, but the New Testament points beyond them to the reality of the demonic world which interacts with these structures, invades them where possible and uses them to maintain its oppressive regime. No analysis of the world or of its redemption is adequate which fails to do justice to this dimension of existence: the tendency of the evangelical tradition to lapse into a world-denying individualism which limits the scope of salvation to the individual soul is to be attributed to this lack of understanding.

When this analysis is applied to the church, light is shed upon the place of the church within society. The church is called to be an expression in the here and now of the kingdom of God, a witness to the kingdom of God which will one day engulf the whole world. As such it is called to live in freedom, not to be enslaved by the principalities and powers of this world. The church is the non-conforming community, not pressed into the mould of this age but inwardly renewed by the Spirit of God, conformed to Christ who is the expression of the will and purpose of God.

But the fact is, the church of Jesus Christ might be extremely sensitive to certain aspects of Christian morality, specifically to personal moral conduct and sexual ethics, while at other points be totally enslaved to the powers of this world. Examples have already been given in relation to South Africa and Northern Ireland of how believers may at the personal level be scrupulously moral but at the level of the 'powers' may be supporting social evil of major proportions. Strange though it may seem to us, previous generations of evangelical Christians not only practised slavery (albeit benevolently!) but actually justified the system of slavery by reference to Scripture. Indeed the arguments they were able to marshal from the Scriptures had considerable force. However devout they were personally, the 'powers' blinded their eyes from seeing something which, to us, is perfectly obvious.

Some aspects of contemporary evangelicalism in the United States of America illustrate the degree to which the powers are able to beguile the church and cause it to conform to their will. The power of nationalism is among the most obvious of these, leading to the identifying of the interests of the kingdom of God with the economic and military interests of the nation. Support for the arms industry and for an increased military budget can therefore be seen as virtuous acts, approved Christian attitudes in the fight against atheistic communism. The degree of corruption inherent in this stance is immense. The Christian is led to deny the New Testament testimony that we are not fighting against flesh and blood and to pervert it into the precise opposite.

The same tendency can be seen as the power of materialism is baptized into the church. The purveyors of the health and wealth gospel proclaim that nothing is too good for 'the King's kids' and that we should do, in God's name, that which Jesus said we should not do, namely set our hearts on treasure on earth. This gospel is nothing more than the incorporation of the American success value into the Christian system. It is congenial and acceptable to those who are already enslaved by the power of materialism, but would no doubt sound somewhat odd in Ethiopia or Sudan, to those enslaved by the power of poverty.

What we are presented with in these two examples is an accommodation of the church to the cultural values of the world. We all underestimate the degree to which we are in fact the product of our class and our culture. We are trained from birth to see the world from the vantage point of our own, or our group's self-interest. It is perhaps only when we travel to a different culture, or begin to see ourselves from the vantage point of another class, or race, or sex, that we begin to grasp precisely to what degree we are being conformed to the powers of our age. A radicalism in the church which is not reflected by a radicalism in the world is no radicalism, or at best is only an easy radicalism.

When Christians have taken Jesus most seriously and have sought to adhere faithfully to the New Testament, they have tended to come into conflict with the powers. This has not been intended on their part. It was not in an attempt to be radical that they became radicals. They were radicals because loyalty to Jesus put them at odds with the established order. The early Christians believed that God had spoken in Jesus and gave absolute allegiance to him as the Christ. This belief brought them into conflict with Rome which maintained an absolutist hold over its subject peoples given coherence by the worship of the emperor. In place of the confession that Caesar was Lord the Christian confessed that Jesus was Lord and in so doing engaged in a political act because he thereby denied the absolute authority of the emperor. It gave the emperor a relative importance, since all authority was of

God, but it denied that the emperor possessed ultimate sovereignty. Although intended as a confession of faith, to confess Jesus as Lord was inherently political in that it confined the 'power' of government to a lesser role and denied it the absolute position which it has so often wanted to arrogate to itself. The Christians were thus seen as a potentially dangerous presence in the empire. For this reason they were persecuted and feared. Their religious confession was politically radical.

A further result of the spread of Christianity was a social radicalism. Even in the pages of the New Testament we can see how the social barriers of the first century were being crossed in the church. The barriers between Jew and Gentile, slave and master, male and female were all transcended by the new social reality of being 'in Christ'. Again, the church represented a threat at this point to the established order of vested interests. It was only as the 'powers' began to reassert themselves over the church that the original dynamism of Christianity was threatened. As we have seen, the legalization of the Christian faith under Constantine left the door wide open for the invasion of the church by the very powers the church itself had once threatened. The church has been seeking to recover ever since.

The Anabaptists were a further example of the radicalism in relation to the political or social order which is a result of the willingness to obey Christ. This time the power was the religio-political hybrid we call the sacral state which was the issue of the Constantinian settlement. As the Anabaptists articulated their alternative system of values they too were harried by the sword because what they were saying struck a blow at the very root of society as it was then constituted. They were feared because of the social and political implications of their convictions.

Where Jesus Christ has been taken most seriously the church has tended to represent a threat to the status quo and to the vested interests of the powers. Where Jesus is proclaimed as Lord the powers are shown to be of only relative and not absolute importance. As the lifestyle of Jesus has been taught and explained, the ways and doings of the powers have been called into question and to a place of servanthood, not of dominion. The powers have sought to counter this first by downright opposition and, when this has failed, by a policy of domestication. What the original persecution against the church failed to do was amply achieved by its legalization. What the persecution of the Anabaptists could not achieve was brought to pass in the fullness of time by the removal of persecution and the arrival of prosperity. History teaches that what the church needs to fear most is not the opposition of the powers but their approval. The danger for the church in the West at this time is that of being beguiled into the service of the powers—religious, political, social and intellectual—and of failing in the service of its Lord.

Jesus, the ethical norm

How does the theme of restoration relate to these things? It causes us to look for our norms of ethical behaviour not in what the powers might persuade us is right but in the New Testament and specifically in Jesus who is God's norm for our lives. It is here that our problems begin, since Jesus is not an easy person to follow. So much is this so that even many who have wanted to confess him have found it hard to take him as the norm for all their moral behaviour.

There are various ways in which the challenge of Jesus can be avoided. It is possible to make the major appeal for principles of behaviour by working back from Jesus to the teaching of the Old Testament with its revelation of the moral law. Thus Jesus is illustrative but the law is normative for behaviour. It is equally possible to work forward from Jesus to the other writings of the New Testament and find ethical norms in the letters of the apostles. Thus Jesus is understood via the other ethical demands of the New Testament. In the task of interpreting Scripture, priority is given to something other than Jesus, whereas it is vital that we interpret the rest of Scripture in the light of Christ. It is possible to say that Jesus was not attempting to give a social ethic, that his commands govern the personal conduct of individual believers, but are not to be applied to society generally. Behind these approaches to the ethics of Jesus is the attempt to wrestle with the implications of Jesus' teaching for us. There is also in good measure the feeling that what Jesus asks of us is so impossible that we have no idea what might happen if we actually did all that he said we should do.

This is where the crux of radical obedience to Jesus is to be found. Do we or do we not believe that Jesus is the norm for the personal and social behaviour of both church and world? It is difficult to see how Jesus can be anything other than precisely this. To establish this point we refer to the doctrines of creation, revelation and incarnation.

Creation

A true Christian doctrine of creation needs to begin not with Genesis but with New Testament affirmations about Jesus' role in creation such as the following: 'Through him all things were made; without him nothing was made that has been made. In him was life, and that life was the light of men' (Jn 1:3–4) and 'For by him all things were created: things in heaven and on earth, visible and invisible, whether thrones or powers or rulers or authorities; all things were created by him and for him' (Col 1:16).

According to the witness of the New Testament, Jesus is the agent of creation. The world was made through him and for him. Jesus, we are told, *is* life and therefore the whole of life can only be properly understood in relation to him. The universe revolves around Jesus Christ. When we seek to have it any other way the result is chaos and confusion. This is as true of the social and political spheres as it is of anything else. We can only grasp the true nature of social and political activity in relation to Christ. For this reason alone, and for many others, to say that religion and politics should be kept apart is a misunderstanding of the nature of existence.

Revelation

Jesus is God's Son, the very Word of God and in him God has revealed himself as he is. 'In the past God spoke to our forefathers through the prophets at many times and in various ways, but in these last days he has spoken to us by his Son . . . The Son is the radiance of God's glory and the exact representation of his being' (Heb 1:1–3). 'He is the image of the invisible God' (Col 1:15). In Jesus we see exactly what God is like. His nature, his will, his ways and his purpose are here disclosed to us definitively. In this way Jesus must be the norm for all human behaviour since there is no higher authority than God and no other source for knowing what is right and what is wrong.

Incarnation

Jesus is the revelation of the true God and in his incarnation he becomes the revelation of the true man. We see in him both what God is like and what man should be like. 'To this you were called, because Christ suffered for you, leaving you an example, that you should follow in his steps' (1 Pet 2:21). 'Follow my example, as I follow the example of Christ' (1 Cor 11:1). If it is the case that in Jesus we see the revelation of the true man then he must be for us the norm and standard for the whole of our lives and for the whole of humanity.

Because Jesus is *the creator*, the one by whom and for whom the world exists, *God's Word*, the revealer of the Father, and *God's incarnate Son*, the revealer of true manhood, he must serve for us as our model and pattern in all things, including our social and political attitudes, actions and behaviour. If we fail to take Jesus seriously at these points we deny the doctrines of the faith.

Jesus and the jubilee

Those who are concerned to follow after Jesus must see the socio-political nature of his message and must be prepared to be faithful to Jesus at these points. Words of Jesus such as these cannot be spiritualized and emptied of their socio-political content: 'The Spirit of the Lord is on me, because he has anointed me to preach good news to the poor. He has sent me to proclaim freedom for the prisoners and recovery of sight for the blind, to release the oppressed, to proclaim the year of the Lord's favour' (Lk 4:18–19). With these words in the synagogue at Nazareth Jesus inaugurates his ministry proclaiming, 'Today this scripture is fulfilled in your hearing.'

Modern scholarship has highlighted the significance of these words from Isaiah 61:1–2 by uncovering their connection with the year of jubilee referred to in Leviticus 25. Every fiftieth year in Israel was designated as a jubilee. In this year the people and the land would enjoy a sabbatical rest, debts would be forgiven, slaves would be set free and every family would return to the original land apportioned to it after the entry under Joshua into the promised land. The effect of this was to be a major upheaval in Israel leading to a radical redistribution of wealth, cancelling of debts and liberation of those who because of debt had sold themselves into slavery. Social justice was the essence of the jubilee, leading to freedom from poverty and oppression.

Transposed into the teaching of Jesus these words became a declaration by him of a new social reality being brought into being in the midst of Israel, a community of men and women living not according to the principles of self-seeking and hostility but on the basis of economic sharing, mercy and forgiveness. It was as this movement began to attract popular support to itself that it became the cause of fear for the religious powers of the Jews and the political power of the Romans. The crucifixion of Jesus has its origin in the counterattack of these vested interests on the new messianic community being formed around Jesus.

Jubilee and the church

The church is the messianic community

In the church which recognizes in Jesus her Messiah, the blessings of the messianic age are to be realized not simply in the forgiveness of sins and the assurance of eternal life but also in economic and social terms in the relations which exist between the members of that community. The essence of this new experience of community is that freedom has been entered into with respect to possessions and anxiety. Life has been seen not to consist in the abundance of possessions, the desire to give is replacing the constant need to gain, self-interest and the acquisitive instinct are giving way to a new experience of generosity. The power of materialism with its attendant anxieties is being eclipsed by trust in God the Father as provider.

As social, religious and cultural barriers are broken down the messianic community becomes a sign that the new age has dawned, it bears its witness to the social justice and righteousness which will be universal when the Prince of Peace reigns in the consummated kingdom. Here is a community which is seeking to resemble the heavenly Father and refuses to take revenge or regard other men and women as enemies. Mercy and love for friend and enemy alike are its hallmarks. Even the oppressive Romans are to be treated with love. In his words and actions Jesus demonstrated the pathway of redemptive love. He walked the way of the cross and refused to do other than love his crucifiers. He called others to take up their own cross and follow him in similar manner. He warned that those who did this would be treated as he was treated.

The messianic community is called to follow Jesus

To say this sounds obvious, but because it costs and may

well lead to the cross we avoid the obvious. The problem with the ethic of Jesus, his call to non-violence for instance, is that we have grave difficulty understanding how it can be applied in our society. What would happen to national defence? What about self-defence? What about defending our families? Because the questions raised have no ready answers we are tempted to evade the words of Jesus and to take our ethical stance in these matters from some other source. We seek to find answers by reference to the interests of our group or nation—by an appeal to 'natural' justice or by repeating the arguments used by those who are strangers to Jesus.

The point for us here is that it is not primarily to the world that these words are addressed, since it is still in the grip of the principalities and powers. It is the church that is first of all called to follow Jesus, since it is we who have experienced the liberation of his rule. It is in the church that the ethic of Jesus must first find its expression and embodiment, and only when this transition in our thinking has been made and we are personally resolved to follow him in everything can we go on to ask, What *forms* of national, self- and family defence (for instance) are consistent with Jesus and his call to us to love our enemies and turn the other cheek? The resolve that is required of us is that of making Jesus our norm for ethical behaviour. *We* must do this before we can bear witness to the world. The issue for the church is one of vocation. It is not that the church is called to avoid the contamination of difficult moral choices—we are all implicated in the world's evil, whatever we think otherwise. It is rather that the vocation of the church is to be the continuing witness in the world to Christ and to his coming kingdom. To do this she must unambiguously follow Jesus and witness to him and his way.

The messianic community is the agent of social change

It is as the church adheres faithfully to Jesus that social change is in fact brought to pass as the result of her witness.

As she bears testimony to Jesus as Lord the powers which claim absolute allegiance from men are exposed and cut down to size.

History itself witnesses to the fact that where a community of Jesus' followers are prepared to embody the life of the kingdom, the impact of that witness upon the wider social structures is not lost. Many of the social advances of the past two millennia have had their origin in the faithful community which has been prepared to suffer for the sake of obedience to Christ. The power of redemptive, suffering love has time and again proved itself. It was, for example, out of the soil of the Anabaptists and later free churchmen that the ideal of religious liberty grew and itself gave life to the growth of the freedoms enjoyed by the western world but still denied to the majority of the human race. Martin Luther King is the most striking modern example of how social change can be purchased at the price of suffering love.

Massive structural reform was achieved by a group of men, inspired by Jesus, who refused to use 'power' and hatred as weapons in the struggle for human dignity. Where such faithfulness to Christ is in evidence, the influence exercised by such a group can be out of all proportion to their numerical strength.

In the English experience, a tiny group of radical Christians such as the early Quakers has contributed positively to the national life at many levels—including fair trading, prison reform and commerce—and to an unusual degree. It is not sufficient to explain such an impact solely in terms of the impact upon conscience that suffering love is able to make. Behind it all is the action of the God who raised the Lord Jesus from the dead and vindicated him because he trusted in him. Where God's people obey Christ and put their faith in God, he will vindicate them, but not without also calling them to experience the sufferings of the Christ.

The challenge of restoration is the challenge of fidelity to the teaching of Jesus in the full awareness that taking Jesus seriously is likely to turn us into nonconformists who at significant points incur the hostility of the powers because of our refusal to conform. The key areas where this is likely to affect us are: in relation to the materialism of our day, since Jesus clearly advocated simplicity and the refusal to amass wealth; in relation to the violence of our day, since Jesus specifically rejected the use of the sword for his disciples in saying 'all who draw the sword will die by the sword' (Mt 26:52) and advocated love of enemies as well as neighbours; and in relation to Jesus' renunciation of the use of power, as was offered to him by the devil, choosing instead to redeem the world by the use of suffering love.

If the church is serious in its intention to follow Jesus, it is not enough to allow our attitudes to these issues to be determined by the 'powers' of our day. If on these issues we do nothing but reflect the prevailing values, interests, opinions and fears of our culture we are not pursuing Jesus to the point of radical obedience. We are avoiding the cost and we are being conformed to the world.

It is not the intention of this chapter to address these issues in detail. This is being done in the publications emerging from the 'radical discipleship' school which follows very much the process of thought engaged in throughout this chapter. Here it is our intention to indicate that the 'restoration' approach to Scripture must be sufficiently radical in its approach to address these questions in the light of Jesus. In so far as it fails to do this, the restoration movement settles for the easy option and betrays the very principle which in other areas it proclaims so boldly.

The most pressing question which is raised for us on this agenda is that of nuclear weapons. By this means our nation, in the name of defence, prepares to destroy, if need be, millions of fellow human beings, including numerous fellow disciples of the Prince of Peace. Both pacifism and the just war theory have an honourable history in the Christian debate over the ethics of war, but it is hard to see how the just war principles can be used to justify the preparation for nuclear war. In the light of all that Jesus stood for, support for the nuclear position seems untenable and may only be justified by appeal to some criterion other than him. Restoration in the church requires us to address this and other issues with the same freedom and fearlessness with which Jesus spoke in his day.

The church and the kingdom of God

How, practically, is the church to function as the agent of the kingdom of God?

By modelling an alternative lifestyle

As it pursues obedience to Jesus above all other values, the church begins to demonstrate alternative beliefs, values and practices to the world. It shows that there are other ways of doing things which actually work better than the world's ways. It demonstrates how needs can be met and conflicts resolved in a spirit of love and service, not one of self-interest and competition. The role of the church is to be exploring the new lifestyle and implementing it for the good of others, that in due time they might be won over to it.

In this sense, the church is the 'avant-garde' of the kingdom of God, it is the people of the future living out the life of the future in the present. Christians are non-rebellious revolutionaries living according to the upside-down values of the kingdom of God modelling the kind of justice, equality, brotherly love and servanthood which will be characteristic of the world when it is restored under the headship of Christ.

By being a witnessing community

The church is more interested in being a witness to the kingdom than in exercising worldly power. The witness is twofold. It is to the principalities and powers and is carried on in the 'heavenlies', that is, it has to do with the invisible world, the realities which stand unseen behind men and nations. By prayer and proclamation of the cross of Christ the powers are dethroned and reminded of their rightful place under

Christ. Demonic entities which have usurped authority are confronted by the Christian community which alone knows how to terminate their rule. The conflict in the unseen world cannot be underestimated although it is impossible to quantify. Even the simple presence of Christians in a community acts as salt and light and is effective out of all proportion to size. The church's witness is also to people, in persuading them—from the base of an authentic and faithful community—to enter into the kingdom and to hasten its final coming as disciples of Christ.

By being both an involved and a non-involved community

The church has no right to retreat into a world-denying pietism. Both through the doctrine of creation which proclaims the goodness of the created order and the doctrine of redemption which holds out the hope of the restoration of all things, the church is world-affirming and must not concern itself with religious matters only. It is called to address the totality of life, therefore the church is for the world and not against it. But it must concern itself with the world not as those who are held by the world but as those who (precisely because they have been freed from it) are able to serve it. The church will therefore be conscientiously involved in the world at those points where it is able to affirm and extend the good but it will also be conscientiously non-involved at those points where its witness to Christ would be impaired, and it will all the time be exercising the gift of discernment in order to tell the difference.

The mission of the church is to call all things in creation to accept voluntarily the rule of Christ now, towards the day when all things will be subject to him. It is both to convert people to Jesus and to 'Christianize' the powers, that is recall them to their proper function in the service of Christ and of the humanity for which he died. Most Christians have some idea about the task of evangelism and a degree of commitment to it, but most will have to learn about the task of witnessing to the powers and seeing them also converted to Christ.

8

Restoration: Freedom, Love and Power

In this chapter we will address three issues which are evoked by observation of the current restoration movement. These are not to be construed as criticisms so much as probings of the extent to which restoration has been faithfully fulfilled at this point in time.

Because of the diverse nature of the restoration movement, it is possible to find different churches stressing precisely the opposite points of view apparently deduced from the same premiss. The reason for this is partly to do with our humanity and partly to do with the variety of emphases which are to be discerned at different places in Scripture, but it means that no set of evaluations of the restoration movement is going to be true of all groups at all points.

It is also good to remember that because God's blessing is upon us, we should not deduce that he necessarily approves of all we are doing. It is the nature of God to be gracious and to bless in spite of our inadequacies or inaccuracies. He will bless all who honour his Son, however wide they may be of the mark at specific points. To argue 'we must be right because God is blessing us', is to misunderstand the nature of grace. Rather we should understand that none of us is exempt from the costly discipline of examining our beliefs, values, practices and attitudes in the light of Jesus Christ.

Restoration and freedom

We have already seen that as an expression of dissatisfaction with the quality of discipleship and discipline in the church, new structures have been given prominence to remedy this. Rebellion against God's appointed authority has been re-established as a grave sin and 'independence' of thought and attitude have come to be regarded with suspicion. Whereas this re-emphasis has the strong merit of highlighting the need for all believers to be accountable to one another, it says nothing about Christian freedom or at best it sees the freedom of the Christian as something to be conceded rather than affirmed, promoted and defended.

If we are to be faithful to the New Testament, freedom must be prominent in our whole set of beliefs, values and practices: 'It is for freedom that Christ has set us free. Stand firm, then, and do not let yourselves be burdened again by a yoke of slavery' (Gal 5:1). The liberating Christ has redeemed his people from their bondage to guilt, sin and death and has opened up a new creation. He has destroyed the work and yoke of the devil and taken captive the powers that seek to dominate and enslave mankind. This all Christians believe and accept. Not so many understand that one of the central facets of freedom is freedom from the law and that this is what Paul had in mind when he wrote his great words on freedom.

The central struggle of the early church was to do with the relationship between Jews and Gentiles in the church of God and it was to resolve this issue that the first council of the church was held at Jerusalem (Acts 15). Gentile believers in Antioch had been disturbed by the teaching of some conservative Jewish believers that in order to be saved they needed to be circumcised and that Gentiles needed to become Jews in order to become Christians. At Jerusalem it became evident that this view was held by Jewish believers of the party of the Pharisees. Their argument was that Gentiles would not be acceptable to God and therefore not acceptable to Jewish believers in the church unless they were conforming to the law of Moses. Throughout his ministry Paul fought against this mentality perceiving it accurately as bondage. It is not that the moral law could be set aside as not valid but that the standing of a believer before God and man was not dependent on outward acts but on faith in Christ. To capitulate to this attitude was to return to spiritual slavery.

For us this discussion may seem remote until we realize that when we judge one another on the basis of outward acts or practices, we are falling into the same error as the Pharisees who imparted their attitudes to Christianity. When we regard certain believers as 'kosher' and others as 'non-kosher' because, for instance, they do or do not speak in tongues, have house groups, practise 'shepherding', submit to an apostle, believe in restoration and so on, we have departed from grace and are beginning to live in law.

In Christ God accepts us apart from any achievements of our own. In accepting us he also renews us inwardly and changes our hearts so that we begin to obey him not on the basis of a set of rules and regulations but because of an ability to discern between right and wrong. It is the conscience redeemed and informed by the Holy Spirit and the revelation of Christ that guides the Christian and that conscience is not to be enslaved to legalism or to the expectations of a group but to Jesus only.

The issue of freedom of conscience was crucial for Luther who insisted on the right of the Christian to deal directly with God's word and not to be dictated to by the pope. It was also crucial for the early Anabaptists who insisted on being obedient to God and his word without waiting for the secular authorities to give them permission. Their conscience did not belong to the town council but to God. It was crucial to the early English separatists who migrated to America in search of such freedom and it is out of this soil that the freedoms of the western world have grown.

More importantly still, this freedom is well-rooted in Scripture. Paul announced the principle in Romans 14:4, 'Who are you to judge someone else's servant? To his own master he stands or falls.' This verse occurs in a passage where Paul is discussing differences of belief over 'disputable matters' (v.1), such as sabbath observance (v.5) and the eating of certain kinds of food (vv.2–3). The burden of the passage is that believers should grant one another freedom before God to do what each believes is right. The issue for Christians is not uniformity of belief or practice but the maintaining of a good conscience before God.

Wherever forces are at work which lessen this freedom, whether in old established institutions or newer ones, we do well to be concerned not only for the health of the church but for that of society, since society ultimately takes its lead from the church. Authoritarian forms in church life will pave the way for authoritarian forms in society. Coercion in any form which seeks to override or undervalue conscience is not in accord with Christ, the New Testament or the vision of restoration. Coercive power is not restricted to the use of legal powers but includes group pressure, the power of personality and the fear of man. Wherever these are employed to create conformity in a church community we have departed from the way of Christ. He does not need those methods to achieve his purpose and neither do we.

To affirm freedom of conscience in the church is to affirm the right of personal judgement. Leaders may advise, inform and guide their people but cannot dictate to them. Individuals must be left free to direct their own lives under God even if this means that mistakes are made. It also affirms the right for the individual to interact with Scripture and to interpret it for themselves. The duty of the church is to uphold and enhance this freedom.

In church terms the corporate equivalent of the freedom of conscience has been known as 'the autonomy of the local church'. By this is indicated not the independence of the local body of believers from any others or their isolation from the wider church, but the freedom of the local church to discern for itself the will and purpose of God. In so far as the development of translocal, apostolic relationships locates authority outside the local church and in an individual with the right to 'rule' over the church, the church is deprived of its freedom. Apostolic ministries should function as enabling and resource ministries, serving the local body and helping it come to an understanding of God's purpose for it, but not depriving it of its corporate freedom to judge for itself.

The task of all of us in the church is to form a body which is wedded to Jesus Christ and not to man. If we are to be faithful to Jesus and the New Testament the issue of freedom must be given greater prominence and emphasis among us.

Restoration and love

To argue that love is portrayed by Jesus as the norm for his church is superfluous. To seek to discover how love and the unity of the church are to be understood is another matter which takes us to the heart of the tensions which exist in the contemporary church. For many in the established, institutional churches the concept of restoration is seen as being divisive both in principle and in practice. In the debate between the 'state' church and 'free' church concepts the ground has now shifted. Those who belong to the 'state' church tradition see their concern to be not the preservation of an established church integrated into the fabric of the nation but the preservation of a degree of unity and of historic continuity in the church as a whole against the ever-present tendency to fragment. Restoration seen from this angle represents a tendency destructive of the unity of the church and disrespectful of its heritage as new churches are continually forming not over central issues but over the latest shade of truth to be rediscovered. Thus the self-indulgent search for a perfect church takes precedence over the need for the church to be one. Evidence of the divisive effect of restoration abounds. Churches divide or are depleted as new churches come into being and, not infrequently, restoration churches divide and so the fragmentation of the body of Christ goes on.

On the other side of the conceptual divide, the restorationists point to the compromise not only of the state church but of the by now heavily institutionalized 'free' churches. Spiritual apathy, traditionalism, non-biblical structures, mixed memberships of regenerate and non-regenerate, theological unorthodoxy in high places all provide grist for the mill. Armed with clichés such as 'moving on', 'being in all that God is doing', 'finding God's man for the area' the restorationists urge those in the Babylon of institutionalism to return to Zion and so hasten the day of the Lord. In this way it comes to be that secession, leaving one church for another, is seen in noble, almost heroic terms.

To add further spice to this recipe we have the spectre of 'denominationalism'. Because the denominations are not of God, since he never instituted them in his word and they are the creation of man, we are duty-bound to oppose them and belong to none of them. To others this argument sounds like saying, 'Because all denominations are not of God let's leave the one we are in and start a new one.' If you want to start a heated discussion with a house-church leader all you have to do is suggest that he is starting a new denomination!

How do we chart a path through the minefield we have just described? We must begin by recognizing what a totally pathetic picture of the church emerges. Whatever we may be able to say in due course of a constructive nature, we must begin by admitting the involvement of us all in the failure of the church. The responsibility for the state of the church cannot be levelled at any one group. The unwillingness of the established churches to change and respond to the work of the Spirit is matched by the massive spiritual pride of the newer churches when they imagine that they are the fullest expression there is of what God is doing. We cannot shake off our complicity in the failure of the total church by ourselves belonging to a section of it which may happen to be, or imagine itself to be, purer than the rest. If the church at any point is displeasing to God we all have responsibility to repent and to grieve.

It has surely to be admitted that denominations are not an expression of the will of God. The only two dimensions of the church witnessed to in the New Testament are the universal and the local. Forms of the church which come anywhere in between these two are lacking a biblical mandate. The only basis on which they might be justified is on that of 'association', that is, the need of groups of churches to associate together for the purpose of mutual service and extension. In the debate about denominations, however, much depends upon our definition of what a denomination is. If a denomination can be defined in legal terms as a group of churches which are legally incorporated into a central body, then 'restoration' churches may justly claim to be outside the denominations for as long as they avoid such legal connections with each other. On the other hand, if it is argued that what creates a denomination is an attitude whereby a certain group of believers distinguishes itself from the remainder of the church and feels itself to be more biblical, faithful, sound or pure over against the rest, then the restoration movement is as much a denomination as any and possibly more so.

What creates denominations is a sectarian attitude such as that evidenced in the Corinthian church where they were setting themselves off over against one another: 'One of you says, "I follow Paul"; another, "I follow Apollos" . . . still another, "I follow Christ." Is Christ divided?' (1 Cor 1:12–13). The root of denominational division is to be located precisely in this attitude and as such, on present showing, the bulk of the contemporary restoration movement offers us not a radical break with the past, but more of the same sin that has bedevilled the church from the beginning and in which we are all implicated. Is there a way out? Yes there is. What follows is an attempt to chart a positive pathway.

The principle of restoration is not inherently divisive

Whatever may have been the practical outworking of the restorationist approach in some—or possibly many—situations, the principle of restoration is not itself a divisive principle since it recalls us to the New Testament theology of the church where we are presented with a vision of unity. Only one flock is envisaged in Scripture and therefore those for whom Jesus and the early church are the norm and measuring rod will pursue that vision because they believe in the restoration of the church along these lines. Where this is lost sight of, the principle of restoration has also been lost sight of. In the best and highest sense restorationists are ecumenists, concerned for the wellbeing of the whole body.

God loves and accepts the whole church

The church is the body of Christ. Wherever men and women believe sincerely in Jesus Christ they are acceptable to God on the basis of the merit of Jesus Christ and not on that of their correct religious practices, church structures or even of their sound doctrine. God is gracious and freely accepts those who come to him in Christ. As we are called to be imitators of God, Christians are called to accept one another unreservedly on the basis of Christ alone. He is our peace. We are called to love what God loves and he loves his whole church. When we fail to do this we are claiming to know better than God himself. We are not called to judge one another but to accept one another. This does not solve the issues of doctrine and practice which remain to be resolved among believers, but it does radically transform the way such issues are approached and addressed. Our wholehearted acceptance of one another is not dependent on agreement but on Christ. To approach one another on any other basis is to fall into the legalism and Pharisaism against which Paul battled and to set ourselves above the Lord himself.

The reality of the love and grace of God towards the whole church is evidenced by his willingness to bless those who seek him. This is not to be taken as proof of his approval of all that is done and said by any particular group but of his grace and mercy which transcend our shortcomings. The basis of unity in the church of God is not common doctrine, practice or ministries but the discernible presence of Jesus Christ among his people.

Respect for conscience allows for differences of approach

The church will never realize its unity until we learn to respect one another's consciences and to give one another the freedom to do things differently. If unity is to become a reality it is not going to happen as the result of man's manoeuvring. It can only be a work of the Spirit of God. What is required of us is the will to be one with all who confess the name of Jesus and in whom he dwells. We need to face the fact that conscience will require different things of different people and whether we agree with the way our brother views a matter or not, we are bound to grant him the freedom so to do.

In applying this to the church of today, there are those who for conscience' sake will feel obliged to move from one church to another, not because they are rebellious or divisive, but because they have genuinely undergone a shift in their understanding of the church which integrity requires them to pursue. Equally there are those whose conscience will lead them to remain in a denominational context, the shortcomings of which are fully obvious to them but within which they feel called to exercise their witness. Doubtless, also, people will from time to time make the shift from one of these positions to the other. The point here is that whichever of these actions may be judged to be correct, the unifying factor that links them is that of a good conscience.

The question which lies beyond this is, Could it be God's will for two persons to follow different courses of action when faced with the same choice? The answer to this must be Yes. If the ultimate end God has in view is the restoration of the whole church and the submission of the whole of its life to Jesus as Lord, this objective may be pursued along different lines.

For some it will involve the liberal, reformist avenue of living within an established church structure while seeking to move it along biblical lines towards the goal of renewal and restoration. This approach will tend to require patience and the ability to accommodate to short-term inconsistencies. The limits of this approach are the limits of a good conscience. Where conscience is compromised this approach cannot be pursued.

For others the renewal of the church will involve a radical, restorationist approach whereby more biblical modes of church life are brought into being and their effectiveness demonstrated. These will in turn become a goad and stimulus which makes for change in the established churches, acting as a catalyst for their renewal.

Along these lines it is possible to look and hope for a massive forward movement in the church of Christ while allowing for differences of tactics. Given a willingness to respect conscience and to avoid judgemental attitudes and given a recognition that the unity of the church is only achieved by recognizing Jesus in one another, there is also hope that the unity of the church in Christ may actually be visibly demonstrated in this process.

Before leaving this section, it may be helpful to point out that this approach, which allows for different tactics, is not without New Testament support. The nature of the major debate within the early church touched on this area, since it had to do with the tension between Jewish Christians continuing to live within the institutional structures of Judaism and Gentile Christians who were setting those traditions aside. The triumph of the council of Jerusalem (and, incidentally, the genius of the apostle Paul) was that both groups were enabled to live conscientiously in Christ and were able to extend mutual recognition to one another while also recognizing different spheres of ministry. Paul himself managed to move from group to group living as a Jew among the Jews and a Gentile among the Gentiles.

The church is moving towards an organic unity

Humanly speaking, to assert that the church will one day be united sounds preposterous. When Christians of the same tradition and inclinations actually find it hard to be at one, what hope is there of a unity which embraces *all* the historic streams and traditions of the church? If there is such a hope it is not to be rooted in the church itself but in the prayer of Jesus for the church that it might be one (Jn 17) and in the vision of the church as a bride adorned for the coming of her Lord (Rev 19:7). Only God can bring this about and the testimony of Scripture is such that we are entitled to hope for its fulfilment.

To conceive of the visible unity of the church as a goal to which we are moving allows room for the work of renewal, reformation and restoration to embrace the whole church and to have its effect. At this time we may only guess at the full implications of this work and at its exact future shape. All Christians will need to be changed and changed again in the process: when it comes the unity of the body will be organic rather than organizational, spontaneous rather than forced, God-given rather than humanly engineered.

Conceiving of the unity of the church in such 'eschatological' terms—that is as a future event—also enables us to understand how it is that we should regard the distinctive elements of witness that belong to the free church tradition. Believers' baptism, the believers' church, church discipline and other features of the radical church are not to be seen as elements that make it superior to others but as truths which are to be held in trust by one part of the church for the sake of the whole church against the day when the whole church will be ready to receive them. In many ways, this process is already at work and many 'established' churches hardly differ, to all intents and purposes, from their radical counterparts. This is because they have become conformed to the Scriptures at these points by being exposed to these Scriptures and to the witness of other churches who have pioneered their application.

The bearing of this testimony to the whole church is to be fulfilled not in triumphalism but in servanthood and is to be accompanied by a willingness to receive the witness of other traditions, to assimilate into our own life that which they are holding in trust for us and so to be mutually enriched. In this way faithfulness to truth as we conceive it need not be perceived as a barrier to unity but as a stimulus towards it. We simultaneously embrace our fellow Christians unconditionally while remaining true to the perceptions of truth that have been entrusted to us; in this way we serve the whole church by both loving it and witnessing to it.

One of the characteristics of the radical free church tradition has been that of sectarianism, the tendency to divide into parties and groups which adopt judgemental attitudes towards each other and towards the wider church. It is this attitude which is the root of denominationalism and which is offensive to God. Sectarianism loses sight of Christ and focuses its attention upon lesser issues of doctrine or church order—it becomes more concerned with form than with function, with correctness than with effectiveness. Sectarianism is a spirit, a mental attitude which grips people, possibly without their even being aware of it. It defiles the body of Christ because it strikes at its unity.

Whereas the bulk of the current restoration movement is motivated by a sincere desire to obey Christ, there are also elements of sectarianism within it, some of which have been inherited from previous such movements and now recycled with a new charismatic garb. If this movement is to be true to the principle upon which it is founded—the recovery of the New Testament vision of the church—it must remove from its life every tendency in this direction and see itself not as the finest expression of church life which can be found but as the servant of the whole body of Christ with which, whether we like it or not, we are all indissolubly joined.

Restoration and power

We have touched from time to time upon the powerlessness of Jesus and his church. By this has been indicated the truth that Jesus did not use worldly or coercive power to bring the kingdom of God and that these means are illegitimate for the church. Wherever the church seeks to establish itself by such means it becomes compromised and corrupted. The renunciation of the use of worldly power sets the scene, however, for the display of a different kind of power—the power of God. It is in order that God's power might be made manifest that the church avoids the use of worldly power or coercive methods.

In his powerlessness, Jesus was anointed with the power of the Holy Spirit. He drove out demons, healed the sick and raised the dead as signs of the presence of God's kingdom. The essence of the kingdom of God is his rule over willing subjects; its sign is the dramatic intervention of God in situations of human need, reversing them in a way which causes people to recognize the presence of the holy in their midst.

The power of God was demonstrated by the resurrection of Jesus after his crucifixion by the principalities and powers, and by the victory enacted and proclaimed in this way. Jesus trained his disciples, gave them authority to do his works and on the day of Pentecost the Spirit was poured out upon them with dramatic and visible results.

This pattern was repeated in the book of Acts with new visitations of the Holy Spirit upon the same disciples, then upon the Samaritans, upon Cornelius and his household, upon the disciples of John in Ephesus and at other points. The picture in Acts is of a church borne along by the Spirit, experiencing the conversion of multitudes, angelic intervention, vision, healings, raisings of the dead, supernatural guidance, trances inspired by the Spirit, supernatural protection and amazing growth.

We have argued in chapter three that we are to see this as normative and not exceptional. It has always been God's intention that such power be experienced among us. If it is not yet our experience we should locate the reason for this not in a theological doctrine but in the state of the church, weak as she is in faith, hope and love. The unbelieving and divided condition of the church quenches and grieves the Holy Spirit.

Charismatic renewal over the past twenty years has not, as yet, resulted in the adequate restoration of the power of the Holy Spirit to the church. It has made an immense contribution to the deepening, broadening and renewing of worship, experience and church life, and this has produced steady growth in many churches. However, we still await the recovery of that kind of power which will be confirmed by signs and wonders and which will result in massively effective evangelism. Perhaps this is another way of talking of revival; whichever way, we need it.

So far the thrust of this book has been to do with our expectations. Do we believe that the vision of the church presented in the New Testament should serve as our normative guide for the church today? Do we believe that the renewal, reformation and restoration of the church is possible along these lines? We have sought to answer in the affirmative and to indicate the areas in which costly change must take place for us all. We do not imagine however that striving to get it right in the church will of itself result in the visitation of the Holy Spirit. History indicates that where the free church principles outlined in this book have been adopted, the church has grown and the missionary impetus has increased. We may argue that such forms of church life as we have described are useful to the Holy Spirit and conducive to growth, but the growth of the church and the fulfilment of its mission will only be accomplished in so far as the Holy Spirit freely and sovereignly brings them to pass. 'Faithful' forms of church life will not persuade the Holy Spirit to act, but brokenness and a sincere seeking after him will not go without a response from the heart of God, since God is the God of grace and mercy. What other attitudes are necessary in seeking after God for the restoration of power?

Honouring the Holy Spirit

J. I. Packer has written, 'Honouring the Holy Spirit has, I believe, been the secret of every revival movement in Christendom from the start' (*Keep in Step with the Spirit*, page 237). Having been the forgotten person of the Trinity, the Holy Spirit of God has more recently been restored to his rightful place in our minds as the one who imparts to us the fullness of God in Christ. The historic theology of the church and our rich heritage of hymns make it clear that Christians worship the Holy Spirit as God.

Strangely, some latter-day Christians are intimidated by the suggestion that we should honour the Holy Spirit in this way. They speak of 'imbalance', they fear excess, they hesitate lest to give more honour to the Spirit is to give less honour to the Son. They are quick with the reminder that the work of the Spirit is to glorify the Son and therefore where prominence is given to the Spirit this surely cannot be of the Spirit. Apparently the Holy Spirit should be kept decently in the background, only being referred to in subdued ways.

Undoubtedly the Spirit's ministry is to bring us to Christ, as surely as Christ's ministry is to bring us to the Father, but it is a strange theology indeed which imagines that we bring glory to the Son of God by dishonouring his Spirit. Against this must be placed the evident and passionate concern which Jesus himself had for the honour of the Holy Spirit: 'And so I tell you, every sin and blasphemy will be forgiven men, but the blasphemy against the Spirit will not be forgiven. Anyone who speaks a word against the Son of Man will be forgiven, but anyone who speaks against the Holy Spirit will not be forgiven, either in this age or in the age to come' (Mt 12:31–32).

The point is this: we honour the Holy Spirit because he also is God and when we honour him we are honouring his work of glorifying the Son. The more the Holy Spirit is honoured the more he will be free to do his work of glorifying Jesus Christ among us. When we are careful in our lives and in our worship to provide a context in which the Holy Spirit is reverenced, loved, worshipped and welcomed then he will do what it is his specific ministry to do, he will take the things of Christ and he will show them to us.

Receiving the Holy Spirit

The debate over the 'baptism of the Holy Spirit' has been one of the most contentious of the last few decades. The debate has centred around two issues: Is it correct to use the term of anything other than the experience of regeneration? and, Should the experience of 'baptism in the Spirit' be linked with the gift of tongues as its initial evidence?

The concern of those who contend that baptism of the Spirit is regeneration is not just one of biblical interpretation. To deny baptism of the Spirit to some and ascribe it to others is to come close to stating that there are two *kinds* of Christians who are to be radically distinguished from one another. This poses immense problems.

On the other hand, the concern of those for whom baptism of the Spirit is to be distinguished from regeneration is that we might fall into the folly of believing that, once regenerate, there is nothing else we need seek, since we 'got it all' at conversion. The legitimate question is posed, If you 'got it all' at conversion, where is it? To affirm the post-conversion reality of baptism in the Spirit indicates that there is more that I need to seek after and to enter into. The fact that I have found God does not mean I no longer need to seek him.

The battleground over this issue has been fought and re-fought. Both sides are able to appeal to Scripture, one finding particular support in Paul's theology and the other in that of Luke. The battle lines are sometimes surprisingly drawn. A prominent charismatic such as David Watson argued against the term 'baptism of the Spirit', preferring to speak of being 'filled with the Spirit'. Not a few charismatics now speak of possessing an evangelical theology with a charismatic experience. Some non-charismatics, such as Dr Martyn Lloyd-Jones, on the other hand, were emphatic about the need to distinguish between regeneration and baptism in the Spirit. In doing this Lloyd-Jones was drawing upon the honourable history of the term in Welsh Presbyterianism to denote the visitation of the Holy Spirit. It is significant that Wales is no stranger to revivals. It was his plea that what the church needed more than anything else was to be baptized with the Holy Spirit and with power.

The debate over the issue is no longer clear cut and easy. No doubt intermingling with the valid points raised there are also on either side less worthy motives, an unwillingness perhaps to acknowledge spiritual poverty, or a defending of an experience for egotistical reasons.

One solution to the complex nature of the debate is to circumvent it and in place of an exclusive approach which says the answer lies with one side or another, to adopt an inclusive approach, which agrees that both sides are right. The baptism of the Holy Spirit is *both* regeneration and subsequent visitations of the Spirit of God. The definitive coming of the Holy Spirit at conversion needs to be repeated in further comings of the Holy Spirit to the believer and the church. When the Holy Spirit comes to us at conversion he comes baptizing into Christ, loosing us from sin and for holiness, equipping and mobilizing us for service, sealing us and adopting us into God's family, and when subsequently he comes and comes again in visitation he does not come to do anything substantially different from what he did at conversion. He comes instead to intensify, to increase, to extend that into which he brought us when we first believed.

This approach has the merit of affirming the identity and unity of all believers while recognizing that there is *more*, and that this *more* can only be brought about by the Spirit of God. To believe that we need more of the Holy Spirit in no way denies the reality of what we have already received but clearly indicates that we need more of the same, more of Christ.

Another way to express this is to say that we received the Holy Spirit at conversion but that we need to go on receiving him. That this was the experience of the early Christians cannot be in doubt. The same believers who received the Holy Spirit on the day of Pentecost in Acts 2 received him again in Acts 4. The Holy Spirit is not to be conceived of as if he were a static possession, but as a dynamic person who indwells us but who also comes to us at specific times and for specific purposes. Indeed the New Testament knows nothing of the 'baptism of the Spirit' as a noun as if it were a thing we possessed. It speaks always of a verb, a baptizing, a process in which we move and are caught up.

Understood in this way, we are confronted by the need of the church to pray for the coming of the Holy Spirit, not to do an alien work but to renew and increase that which is his own work, the conviction of sin, the impartation of life and power and the glorifying of Jesus Christ in all these things. Until and unless the church learns to do this, we will not be true to the New Testament vision of the church.

Freeing the Holy Spirit

The other area of debate over baptism in the Holy Spirit, concerns the gift of tongues as the initial evidence of the Spirit's baptism. This is classic Pentecostal doctrine and suffers from the fatal flaw of seeking to predetermine the way the Spirit's coming will be manifested. It is one thing to say that the Spirit's coming either at conversion or subsequently may be accompanied by the phenomenon of tongues, it is quite another to assert that this *must* happen. When we do this we run the danger of missing what the Spirit of God may actually be doing and this may not match our preconceptions at all. The gracious work of the Spirit cannot be made into law. In this we are highlighting the human tendency to want to control or define the work of the Spirit of God.

Jesus plainly taught that the Holy Spirit is like the wind. He is free and self-determined. His work may be described but cannot be defined since to define it is to limit it to our definition. If the church is to be restored in its experience of the power of the Spirit and his coming, we must settle in our minds that we should let the Spirit be free to do his work. We should recognize with this that there will be times at which we will be surprised—possibly even shocked—at what he does. The Bible and the history of revivals bear testimony to the fact that when the Holy Spirit works in power this may be accompanied by unusual phenomena. Men fall down in the presence of the holy, some are seized by violent trembling, others behave, as on the day of Pentecost, as though drunk. Visions and ecstasies, groanings and loud confessions of sin break out spontaneously. Demons located and hidden in the flesh are exposed and expelled. Individuals break out into tongues or prophecy, into tears or into gladness.

Repeatedly in the book of Acts we are told that the Holy Spirit *fell* on people. The very word implies a degree of suddenness and of force. It is no wonder that those who witnessed this were amazed. Some were offended and scoffed while others believed. It will be no different today when the power falls upon God's people. The Spirit disrupts as well as bestowing peace. He is the wind that blows gently and that which blows like a gale carrying all before it.

The question posed for us by the biblical witness to the Holy Spirit is whether we are actually prepared to let the Holy Spirit be free to do what he wills in the church of Jesus Christ.

Fear of excess is what inhibits many. In the name of 'balance' we tolerate an extreme imbalance which excludes the Holy Spirit from doing what he wills in the church of Christ. Because we fear the unreal we shut out the possibility of the real happening among us. The fact is that where the Spirit is at work he will expose the unreality which already exists in our hearts and in the church. As with Simon there will be those who seek to pervert the ways of God for their own ends but as with Peter there will also be supernatural authority and enabling to deal with the unreal and the ungodly.

To give freedom to the Spirit means exposing ourselves to new sets of demands, new challenges of understanding, and the need to learn how to discern the workings of the Spirit. There is great cost involved in all of this and because of this cost many refuse to allow God the freedom to work in his church in whatever way he chooses. While we limit God in this way we will be strangers to the dynamic power of the early church. Once we resolve to give freedom to the Holy Spirit, honouring his presence in the midst and yielding to him, we will begin to recover what the church has lost and so desperately needs, the visitation of the Holy Spirit.

9

Restoration and the Dynamics of Change

Change in the Bible . . . change in the church

We come in this chapter to the practical issue of how all that has been said so far affects the life of the local congregation. What has been outlined is a vision of the church drawn from the New Testament witness and already well attested in the history of the church. It is a vision of a church renewed and restored in its experience, theology, structures and ethics, functioning powerfully and effectively in the world as the sign and agent of the kingdom of God.

Viewed from the base point of the early church, this vision can spell one thing, the need of today's church to change and to be transformed from being the institutionalized, hierarchical, organizational entity it has by and large become into being a charismatic, Spirit-led organism expressing in all the dimensions of its existence the life of Jesus Christ. What is described in this book is a call for change.

It is at this point that theory should be translated into practice and become costly. Change is painful. All human beings find it difficult. All change is crisis since it removes old securities from us and requires us to face up to challenges we have never met before. It requires extra effort in every area. We have to think more, plan more, talk more, decide more, communicate more and tolerate more. It sometimes spells the laying on one side of institutions or customs in which much loving time has been invested over years. We are asked to believe that a goal towards which we are reaching but have not yet attained is worth all the costly and messy struggling which is our present lot. Change evokes a whole battery of memories and fears, of insecurities and inadequacies. It opens up the door for feelings of rejection and hurt, confusion and uncertainty. Yet precisely this is the challenge of the hour. No change signifies no growth. Where there is growth there will be change. Things cannot stay as they are and also grow and develop.

Before getting down to business it is good to remember that the mandate for continual change is a biblical one. The Old Testament seems to be much at home with the picture of the people of God as the pilgrim people. Delivered from Egypt they were kept constantly on the move led by the pillar of fire and the cloud of God's presence. They had eaten the passover in Egypt with their cloaks tucked into their belts, sandals on their feet and staff in hand, ready for the journey that was to follow. They were kept on the move and were commanded to make a portable tent containing a portable altar as God's dwelling place. Everything spoke of movement, of pilgrimage and temporary residence. It is significant that whereas it was David's idea to build a temple for the Lord, it had been God's idea to have his people make a tent.

God's church is a pilgrim church constantly on the move and always battling against the deflecting influence of institutionalization. History bears witness to the constant temptation for the church, whether conceived of according to the state church or the believers' church model, to settle down where it is and leave off from the pilgrimage of constant renewal and reformation. Many movements which began as radical renewal movements have ended up as bound in tradition and retrospective attitudes as anything against which they were a protest. Radical leaders of the past have ended up as patron saints of the status quo in the present. We must resist the constant temptation to leave off from pilgrimage.

The New Testament also calls us to a life of change. Paul writes: 'And we, who with unveiled faces all reflect the Lord's glory, are being transformed into his likeness with ever-increasing glory, which comes from the Lord, who is the Spirit' (2 Cor 3:18). Change is of the essence of the new covenant. This is not to say that all change that happens is right, or properly managed. But it does indicate that he who resists change may very well be found resisting God. The biblical mandate is one for change; the principle of restoration which calls us back to the New Testament as our point of orientation helps us to spell out the dimensions of that change in personal and corporate terms. He who believes that our basic task in the church is simply to defend what we have inherited has clearly not understood his Bible. While gathering up that which we have received which is good and right, we are called to live open-endedly and to be transformed from one degree of glory to another, moving towards a future and ultimate goal.

This chapter is written from the vantage point of the local church and specifically from a pastoral perspective. In the ferment of change being evidenced in the contemporary scene under the impact of the ideas and concepts already touched upon, many pastors and church leaders have faced, are facing or have yet to face, the challenge of restoration in the local church. The concepts of the believers' church, plural leadership, the power of the Holy Spirit and the like are now informing the approach of thousands to the nature of church life.

In the case of the many who are planting new churches from scratch the challenge is that of establishing healthy principles and practices reflecting New Testament values and theology from the beginning. Those who are in established congregations must face the difficult challenge of edging aside the old while bringing in the new, a feat not unlike that of servicing a car engine or perhaps even reconstructing it while it is still running! That this is no easy task is amply demonstrated by the pain and anguish experienced by so many on either side of the change divide.

The considerations touched upon in this chapter have to do with the facilitating of change in the local congregation by the pastoral leader or leaders. Those who are not in pastoral leadership may nevertheless find it helpful to try and see it from this perspective. The undergirding conviction of these considerations is that change according to the word of God is necessary. Given time most people adapt to change, although at different rates, but some will oppose it resolutely believing that in so doing they are serving God. What are the dominant features of the change process and how can it be facilitated?

Visionary pragmatism

For the church leader whose persuasion is that things in the church are not as they should be and that obedience to the word of God obligates us to move to a better place, two qualities are essential. The first is that of *vision*, namely the ability to be inspired by a sense of the way things ought to be and to inspire others with it.

Moses and the children of Israel endured the privations of the wilderness for the sake of the promised hope set before them. The exiles were sustained in Babylon by the hope of a restoration in Israel. A leader who is himself inspired by a vision which draws him on will also be one who is able to inspire that vision in others.

It is a joyful sign in the church today that a sense of hopelessness about the church is being replaced by an ability to believe for something so much better, leading to a recovery of buoyancy and confidence which themselves make for growth and creativity. The church is not faced with a future of continual decline but with one of vibrant possibilities.

The leaders in the church need to be people who have

committed themselves to the pilgrimage of hope and who are resolutely pursuing the vision and not just bolstering up the past. Shepherds lead the flock into acres of good pasture and they do so not by driving people from behind but by walking in front.

By their nature visions tend to be imprecise. They are difficult to define and analyse, their full implications are not easy to work out. Like Abraham, they involve our setting out not knowing where we are going but believing that in the process of obeying the promptings of God, it will become clear as the pilgrimage unfolds. We may not know the exact meaning or shape of the vision but we have hope that we will recognize its fulfilment when we see it. In the process of change, the sense of pursuing that which lies just beyond the horizon is vital. The need of the church is to be set free from a retrospective, nostalgic perspective obsessed with what was and to embrace a forward-looking, visionary attitude. A holy restlessness which is grateful for both past and present but which eagerly looks to the future is a basic ingredient in church growth. It is as we read our Bibles and confront the vision of the early church, asking the question Why not?, that such a biblical and realizable vision is imparted to us.

The other side of the coin is *pragmatism,* a practical sense of how the vision applies and how much of it is realizable now. The art of leadership is actually to lead people from one place to another. Leaders who are all pragmatism and no idealism are likely to lead nobody anywhere since they do not know where to go. Those who are all idealism and no pragmatism may get to the promised land themselves, or with a small group of others, but leave the bulk of the people behind.

In the leadership process, it is immature to expect too much too soon. A shepherd in biblical times had to be ahead of the flock but not so far ahead that the flock could not recognize his voice and receive direction. Often leaders who have nurtured and considered a vision over a long period of time expect others to respond to it instantaneously and become disillusioned when this does not happen. Those who lead need to understand the right of those who are led to consider the vision and to invest themselves in it. It is possible to push towards a worthy goal at a pace which is far too demanding and to write off those who fail to survive this process as recalcitrants.

Visionary pragmatism is the ability to hold on to a vision but also to judge the pace at which that vision may be pursued without losing touch with those whom the leader is leading. This requires an ability on the part of the leader to exercise patience and to live with inconsistencies and anomalies in the state of affairs as it currently exists, knowing that in due course this will yield to something better.

There will be issues in church life which are matters of conscience, where some basic principle of faith is being compromised and Christian integrity is being violated: in such cases a resolute insistence on repentance and change is in order. But many aspects of church life do not come into this category; they have to do with issues which are lawful but not helpful, with structures which are cultural rather than Christian, with organizations which have lost any anointing they may once have had. In the case of such things, it is unwise to make major issues out of minor points and better to adopt a pragmatic attitude which takes a long-term view.

Rates of change

Human beings adapt to change at differing rates depending on their individual make up. In each congregation there will be a small percentage of 'innovators', people who feel at home with change, who are themselves visionaries able to think themselves into mental models of new forms and structures of church life. Such persons are essential to any congregation in providing new ideas and act as catalysts for the whole.

A larger percentage of people will belong to the 'early majority' who, although not as adventurous as others, will readily adapt themselves to new ideas and new ways without too much difficulty.

Parallel to this group is a roughly equal one in size which constitutes the 'late majority', those who given time, space and encouragement will become reconciled to change and gradually invest themselves in it. These people tend to need to see something in operation before they are able to identify with it, but once persuaded will be firm and resolute.

Finally there are the 'retarders', those who for various reasons are unwilling for change at any price and, although small in number, will exert an influence far beyond their size. Of this group some may with perseverence be won over to change after much prayer and heartache, others will conclude that they are unable to identify with it and will opt out accordingly.

Conceived of in this way, adaptation to change is like crossing a bridge. The innovators will find their way across first, followed by the early majority. When these have safely negotiated the way they will beckon the late majority to join them. The retarders will waver long before attempting the crossing and some will succeed amidst rejoicing, others will conclude that the journey is too dangerous and will turn away.

The interesting feature of this process of change in church terms is that the innovators will by and large not be those who sustain and lead the church in its new changed form. It will be those in the early and late majorities who become the anchor people in the new situation. Innovators by their nature tend to be mercurial and changeable.

In looking at change in these terms, various other factors are discernible. Where an individual is to be found in their willingness to adapt to change will vary according to factors of age, temperament, imagination and experience. Some individuals will move from one group to another in the course of time. Those who innovate and press for change early on may become more cautious later and move into the early or late majority. Some may even make the complete journey from 'innovator' to 'retarder'! Marriages and families may come under pressure when, for instance, an innovator is married to a member of the late majority, or when children press for change beyond the capacity of their parents to cope with it. A member of the late majority in one church might find themselves an innovator on moving to another, or even in one church one who presses for rapid change over one issue might seek to retard it over another.

All these dynamics are at work in any congregation although to differing degrees and over different issues. The pastoral leader needs to be aware of the dynamics of change and of the surprising fluctuations that may take place within the church over a period of years in the willingness of people to support and advocate it.

The key in leading a church through such a time is to know what rate of change to allow and encourage. The leader must lead and cannot surrender that task to others; but leadership consists in knowing when to hold back and delay as well as when to press forward. Leadership does not always mean innovation, but sometimes the restraining of it. To pitch the rate of change too far in the direction of the fastest means alienating the slower and slowest. Conversely to yield to the slowest means alienating the faster and fastest. There is usually a point of consensus which allows of substantial unity in the church being maintained while not smothering the change process and preventing it. The task of the pastoral leaders is to identify this and advocate it with resolution. At different points this will appear either to be too fast or too slow to some but the important contribution of the leaders is to provide a secure rhythm of leadership through change rather like the security of a metronome beating time for an orchestra which fades or swells at different points of a symphony.

One of the characteristic features of a church in the transition of change is that the leadership are caught between two opposing forces, those who are pressing for change and those who are opposing it—or, putting it slightly differently, those who want to go too fast or too slow. In negotiating this difficult stage much depends on the ability of leaders to keep the trust of both sides by listening to and understanding their respective frustrations, fears and struggles. Often, those who press for change are operating under the pressure of an unnecessary anxiety about 'not making it'. Those who oppose change are similarly often gripped with an irrational fear. It is essential to minister to these emotions and to insist that change is necessary but needs also to be change at depth and not just superficially, therefore precipitate, hasty change is counterproductive.

The essential factor in determining the rate of progress is for those who lead to be able to say, 'This is what we believe God is telling us to do next.' If it is fear of man which determines progress then the result will be confusion. If the church is enabled to find the mind of Christ for this church at this time there will be security in charting a forward course.

Aids to change

The change process is facilitated by a number of stimuli which are essential for producing a climate conducive to change.

Preaching

It is by and large true that the shape of the preaching will determine the shape of the church. What is essential is to bring about through the preached word the shift in mentality that will set people on the road towards renewal and restoration. This is done by teaching the New Testament and the fact that it is to be taken as our norm. Preaching which stimulates people's vision by setting goals before them and drawing a picture of what the renewed church is like in the purposes of God will create a hunger to see such a church brought to pass.

It is essential in the process of change to interpret new departures or experiences in biblical terms. As people fear the unknown it is helpful for them to be given explanations of what is happening among them rather like Peter did on the day of Pentecost when he interpreted the phenomena of that day in terms of an Old Testament prophet, saying, '. . . this is what was spoken by the prophet Joel'.

Preaching may be compared to the ploughing process as fallow ground is broken up that a new harvest may be brought forth. Through patient teaching and preaching the foundations are laid for constructive change. This does not mean that all will necessarily go smoothly when the preacher moves from words to action—people can usually take any amount of theory without being unduly threatened by it, but actual change comes as a threat. It does mean, however, that a consensus for change and a consequent dynamic of change are being created through the preached word.

Outside exposure

Part of the resistance to change is simply due to lack of imagination, the inability of people to think themselves into different ways of operating. The change process is aided where people can be exposed to the influence of situations where change has been healthily achieved. This can be done through books, tapes, conferences, Bible weeks, visiting speakers or teams where models of renewal and restoration can be presented and illustrated. Visits to other churches by leaders and others can provide a catalytic effect.

To be sure, people also need to be guarded against the romantic tendency to live in an unreal world without regard to the realities of their own situation. What people have done in other churches can be very intimidating if we are expected to be like them, and so an openness to others must be accompanied by the insistence that our church is unique and must be allowed to tread its own path at its own rate. No church should be the clone of any other.

Another form of outside help is that of apostolic guidance. We have referred to the renewal in understanding of the apostolic, translocal dimension of ministry available to the local church as a resource. The guidance of such a ministry in a transitional period can be of immense help, particularly if such a person has experience and insight in this area. For most churches the problem at this point is that of finding the right person or persons which means someone with whom the church can be relaxed and secure and with whom such a relationship is not a forced, organizational move but an organic, Spirit-inspired one. Not all churches will be able to find someone who fits the bill, but those who can will benefit greatly from the counsel received.

United leadership

If in the dynamics of change, a church is able to keep a united leadership, it will almost certainly remain united as a whole. Ideally, therefore, the task of those in leadership is to work hard at hammering out agreement with one another, understanding each other's point of view and seeking to maintain the unity of the Spirit in the bond of peace. The leaders' task is to model to the whole church how it is possible to walk together in a time of change. Doing this depends heavily on the type and quality of persons in leadership. Where unity is lacking it is best to wait until it can be achieved before pressing on.

Pastoral wellbeing

The person who pays the price for change more than any other is the pastoral leader. It is therefore essential that he should take care to safeguard his own spiritual and personal health. Coping with change produces more stress in pastoral ministry than virtually any other aspect of the work, and takes its toll. Rest and recreation are essential in these times and should be carefully guarded. Great change and great blessing often go hand in hand with the result that the pastoral leader can experience great swings of mood within the course of a month, a week or even a day. The church can look either bursting with health, or on the verge of collapse, according to mood! At this point the pastoral leader stands in need of affirmative relationships both within the church and beyond it and does well if he can seek out those with whom such a relationship is possible. One of the greatest anomalies in the church is that of the unpastored pastor, and it is in response to this anomaly that the growth of peer groups among pastoral leaders and the development of apostolic ministries should be seen.

Pastoral work

At the best of times, there is no substitute in the church for ordinary, regular pastoral work. This is all the more so in times of change.

In recent years there has been a tendency to devalue the involvement of the pastoral leader in 'ordinary' pastoral work, seeing him more as a specialist who involves himself with other leaders, but this is a mistake. It is essential for pastors to be in touch with people and not to be removed from them. This is not to say that others should not carry the regular pastoral burdens but that however many others are mobilized in pastoral service, pastoral leaders should still involve themselves as much as possible in the caring ministry.

In times of change, people tend to become alienated from one another because they are straining in different directions. Regular, diligent pastoral visitation can help cross these gaps and create the kind of trust and confidence that is necessary. Births, marriages and funerals can become times of drawing together, establishing confidence and showing compassion. People cope with change more easily when they feel that their point of view is understood and considered and when they feel they are in touch with those who are in authority. Pastoral leaders need to be ready to bear the pain of hearing people who disagree with them and of absorbing their fears and disappointments.

Resistance to change

Change is difficult to manage even where those involved are all people who act in good conscience and with good will.

Sadly there lurk within most churches resistant forces which are rooted in flesh rather than conscience and which are apt to assert themselves when their dominion is challenged.

Culture and tradition

Churches are more culturally bound than we realize. When we imagine that we do what we do because it is sanctioned by the word of God, the truth is that much that we do is purely cultural and relative. Much church life is the product of the Victorian era rather than Scripture and yet claims an absolute importance. For instance, previous generations of free churchmen strenuously resisted the use of organs in church, preferring the unaided human voice as the instrument of worship rather than 'worldly innovations'; yet once established as part of church life, the organ has become for many the sacrosanct, anointed instrument which God takes pleasure in to the exclusion of all others. Thus relative features of church life are given exalted significance.

Jesus accused the Pharisees of making void the word of God by their traditions; in the church too the traditions of men exalt themselves as of supreme importance thus obscuring the word of God. It is not wrong for the church of God to draw upon the traditions and heritage of the past when they can be made to serve God in the present, but it is totally wrong for the church to be bound by traditions in a way that prevents it from responding to the Spirit. A church in the process of renewal and restoration will inevitably encounter resistance from traditions. Some traditions need to be confronted outright and defeated, others can be eased on one side and allowed to wither away, others may be captured, transformed and employed in the service of the King.

Vested interests

These are akin to traditions. Since we all have a tendency to empire-build, we invest ourselves in activities to the degree that they become 'ours'. Our sense of identity and significance becomes dependent upon the tasks we perform to such a degree that we will defend our territory against change. Every aspect of church life runs the risk of becoming a vested interest and to the degree that it does become so it becomes resistant to the kingdom of God which is opposed to the empire of man.

As a church is renewed in each dimension of its life, the vested interests in each area will be exposed and will squeal. They will counter change with suspicion, hostility and misrepresentation and must in turn be confronted with honesty, patience, love and firmness. It is best to encourage change in these areas in as open a way as possible so that the full dimensions of the need for change and of the resistance to it are clear to as many people as possible. Structures must be kept continually under review with nothing being allowed to become sacrosanct and with everything subject to review on the assumption that what justifies any given structure is its effectiveness in fulfilling its object and purpose. The people of God need to be taught to recognize vested interests for what they are and to name them as such since a church which practises mutual submission cannot support vested interests within itself.

Spiritual forces

In reviewing resistance to change it is important to recognize the reality of spiritual warfare. Demons delight in vested interests and exploit them for their own ends. They will sow fear of change and distort peoples' attitudes to leaders and others who advocate it. They will sow gossip and suspicion into hearts and minds. Because the church is important in God's economy, demonic powers will take the battle into the church itself and will find plenty of opportunities to work their works.

Over and beyond those human skills which facilitate change, the church needs to arm itself with the gift of discernment, with prayer and with the word of authority. We need to learn how to recognize the work of the enemy among us and to bind the power of darkness even as we refuse to become his accomplices by falling into line with it. There will be events and incidents in the history of most churches which need to be repented of in order to break the hold Satan may have on us because of them—acts of unkindness, unresolved quarrels, unloving selfish actions. In addition, there will be influences within the church in the present which displease God and need to be broken. All these are aspects of the spiritual battle which is waged around us unseen but nonetheless real and with which we have to do. To seek to welcome the kingdom of God in our midst is to dislodge spiritual powers which grip both individuals and churches and is to become acutely aware of the spiritual conflict. Leaders will need to fast and pray to remove obstacles not by force of argument or power but in the Holy Spirit.

The cost and the ethics of change

To initiate and manage change in the way that has been described is a costly affair. The pastoral leader faces the possibility of misrepresentation of his motives and actions. He faces the hostility and suspicion of vested interests. He faces the possibility of disappointment as some for whom he has cared reject his leadership and as others who initially were supportive lose courage and withdraw their support. With this goes the possible loss of reputation among colleagues in ministry who may not be sympathetic and begin in ways obvious and subtle to distance themselves. There is the pressure of having to spend much time in exhausting dialogue with others on the way forward over specific issues. Long meetings are a feature of a church in change seeking to wrestle with new thinking and new ways. There is the tension between popularity and obedience since all pastoral leaders are people people and thrive upon the affirmation of others, and yet there are times when to obey God is to become unpopular. For those who have pastoral hearts, to pursue a course of action which others find distressing does not come easily, but although leaders are servants of the people that does not make the people their master. God alone is the master and he alone is to be obeyed.

There is sufficient cost involved in change even when it is well managed that those who set out in this direction need to have an adequately strong vision of what God wants to achieve through them. The cost is all the greater, however, when change is unwisely or even in some cases unethically managed. It is not only important to know where we are going but also to know how we should get there. The end does not justify the means since it is within the means that the seeds of success or failure are contained. In the work of Christ we have to do with people and people should not be lost sight of and sacrificed for the sake of a vision.

A characteristic temptation for pastoral leaders is that of exploiting or manipulating people for the sake of an ambition to produce a church of a certain kind. It is essential both to have a vision and to pursue that vision *through* loving and serving the people, rather than pushing them on one side. It is precisely at this point that many churches intent on restoration have pursued a good vision through an unloving means. Acting under the pressure of an anxiety that they might not make the grade if they fail to 'move on', a pressure intensified by the fear of disobeying God and by authoritative voices to which they have listened, they have sought to bring about by force what can only be achieved by love.

God's work can only be properly achieved through God's own appointed means, which is love for the brethren; to pursue even a good end in any other way is to do violence to the body of Christ. The speed with which we arrive at a renewed, restored church is not as important as the way in which we arrive. Far better to move slowly and arrive with a good conscience than to force the pace and yet do unnecessary harm along the way. This is not to say that difficult decisions will not also need to be taken but it is far better to take these in loving regard for integrity and good conscience than as part of a power struggle which involves coercing others to do things they do not choose to do for themselves. If God is the source of renewal and restoration in the church then he may be trusted to prove faithful to his purposes without the need for us to resort to acts of human power.

The ethics of change involve a refusal to force things upon others and an insistence that everything that is done should be done 'in the light'. It means being true to commitments that have already been made and to procedures, for instance of decision-making, which are already commonly agreed in a church until such a time as new procedures are properly adopted. It requires a refusal to resort to powerful means of forcing through policies since this is the world's way of doing things. It involves a respect for consensus and an attempt to reconcile opposing opinions. Compromise is not wrong when it grows out of love and consideration and when it is concerned with matters for which Scripture does not legislate. For those pursuing the vision of restoration it is essential to pursue the vision in love and through love and in this way the vision itself will become more and more attractive because of the fruit by which it is accompanied.

Because of the cost involved in change and the pressure brought upon pastoral leaders who advocate it, it is a temptation to respond to hostility with hostility or to engage in precipitate or over-assertive activities which bring disrepute upon the cause espoused. Where instead the response to hostility is self-sacrificing love, pastoral leaders will grow in authority and others will be willing to follow them. Conversely, great damage is done to the restoration cause when that cause is pursued in unethical and unrighteous ways.

Restoration and leadership

In this chapter stress has been laid on pastoral leadership in the belief that it is in the dynamics of change that the gift and service of leadership comes into its own. Wise pastoral leaders who can chart a course through difficult waters and yet do so without dominating or forcing others but by the authority and quality of their lives and insight, are essential to a church in the throes of change.

Long-lasting change does not happen overnight since churches are families and families need time to grow and mature and need the presence of fathers and mothers who can be the secure points around which such growth to maturity can happen. Leaders need, therefore, to give time and patience to their church families. They need to be people who are not blown about by every wind of change or carried away by the latest enthusiasm but who know how to listen to God and to hear from him. Such leaders refuse to be intimidated by what others do or say since they know that there is no formula for church life, no one model which is equally valid everywhere. They are visionaries but they are also loving servants who know their people and understand what is and is not possible at any given time. They have the capacity for self-correction since they know that times of change are also times of imbalance. They have the ability to dream, to think, to assess and to enthuse. Among those who lead should be those who have the theological ability to see the whole and not just the individual parts, who can enable the church to avoid unhelpful diversions in the pilgrimage towards the horizon and who can distinguish between those issues which are vital and those which are not. People such as this can turn a potentially traumatic phase of church life into a maturing process which leaves the church not only different but also wise and strong. Such people are the need of the hour.

10

Restoration and the Future

In all that has so far been written we have been referring constantly to the New Testament. It has been argued that the New Testament theology of the church, and the witness to Christ and his church it contains, should be seen as the norm for the church of today. Only in this way can we take the authority of the Bible seriously. This is not to say that the early church was without fault. It is no part of our intention to portray the early church in romantic terms. The struggles, failings and errors to be found in the New Testament era are set before us with astonishing honesty and it was as a corrective to them that much of the New Testament was written. Taking the New Testament as our norm and measuring rod the intention of this book is to orientate us towards the future not to muse nostalgically on the glories of the past. The glory that is to be manifested in the church will surpass that which was known in the New Testament era. The New Testament remains the root and norm of our faith but is to be eclipsed in the fulfilling of that towards which it bears witness.

Future hopes

In recent years, the theme of hope has reappeared in Christian theology with great vigour. According to Paul the three great virtues are faith, hope and love. Faith and love are well understood in the church, even if our practice of them may leave much to be desired. Hope, however, is a neglected virtue. It is that certain confidence and expectation we have concerning the future God has prepared for us; as such, it is of crucial importance since it will shape our motivations. What we hope for will determine how we act and how we spend our lives. Jesus told the parable of the man who found treasure in a field and sold all that he had to purchase the field. His hope of gaining the treasure led him into costly and sacrificial action and he entered into it 'in joy' (Mt 13:44) because of his discovery. What we believe concerning the future will shape our actions in the present and the precise nature of those expectations is vital since they will provide the wellspring for our actions in different spheres.

Unfortunately, eschatology (the study of the last things) has for centuries been a Christian happy hunting ground for fanatics, extremists and the sects. Bizarre interpretations of Scripture and the events of history have brought disrepute upon the enterprise of constructing a theology of the future. Christian credulity has been at its worst in seeking to make sense of the prophetic dimension of God's word. At the root of much of this has been a failure to understand the nature of the prophetic and apocalyptic portions of Scripture. Taken over-literally and sometimes viewed crudely through rationalistic presuppositions the Scriptures have been made to mean things which were never part of the original intention.

To understand the Bible aright in what it says of the future it is necessary to grasp that the revelation comes to us in visionary and symbolic form and not for the most part in literal description. Understanding is a question of knowing the Christ of whom these portions speak, not in finding the right formula for cracking the code.

Prophetic interpretation has tended to hinge around Revelation 20 and the concept of the millennium. In this chapter a reign of Christ on earth for a thousand years is referred to. The question is, When does this millennial reign occur and what does it involve? The various strands of interpretation offered in answer to these questions are as follows.

Premillennialism

According to this view, the return of Christ occurs before his millennial reign. It is when he and his saints reign on earth ruling the nations and restoring the creation to God's original intention. It is a time when the vivid prophetic and this-worldly hopes of the Old Testament are fulfilled and it precedes the new heaven and the new earth. Apocalyptic Jewish thought, which has shaped many of the thought forms of Revelation, expected there to be six thousand years of human history followed by a further millennium corresponding to the sabbath. History would conclude with a period of sabbatical rest under the reign of the Messiah. This way of thinking, it is argued, was adopted by the early Christians.

Modern premillennialism takes two forms. *Dispensational* premillennialism takes a highly literal view of Scripture and is much in vogue today, especially in the United States. It awaits the appearance of antichrist followed by the coming of Christ to initiate a literal reign on earth of one thousand years. *Historic* premillennialism avoids the literalism of dispensationalism but sees the millennium as symbolic of a final period of history in which the kingdom of God will be realized on earth and expressed in human history. Various forms of premillennialism have repeatedly appeared in history mainly among radical groups such as the Anabaptists.

Amillennialism

Amillennialism rejects the concept of a literal reign of a thousand years. It argues that the symbolism of Revelation should not be taken at face value at this point and should certainly not be the hinge on which prophetic interpretation turns. Obscure scriptures are to be interpreted in the light of those which are clear and Paul's specific teaching in 1 Corinthians 15:20–28 makes no mention of a millennium. Rather the coming of Christ is to be followed immediately by 'the end'. Revelation 20 is therefore to be interpreted symbolically of the reign of Christ which is happening now *behind* and *beyond* history. It began with his resurrection and will be made clear at his appearing in glory. This view of the millennium has been the dominant view of Reformed theology and has tended, from the time of Luther and Calvin onwards, to look with suspicion at premillennialism seeing it as the product of fanaticism.

Postmillennialism

Postmillennialism is a minority view which believes that the second coming occurs after Christ's millennial reign, although 'one thousand years' is to be seen as largely symbolic and the actual time scale may be much shorter. This triumphant reign will be brought about by the preaching of the gospel to all the nations. As the gospel has its impact upon the whole world it will bring about righteousness and conversion on an immense scale transforming human society. After an extensive period of victory for the church there will be a short time of apostasy prior to the coming of the Lord and the end.

This view was held extensively by the seventeenth-century English Puritans and is credited by some as providing the impetus for the dramatic spread of Christian missions from the eighteenth century onwards. It is seen as having generated a confidence and optimism about what was possible *now* through the preaching of the gospel which led to the bold endeavours of the great missionary movements.

Assessing the hopes

Each of these positions has its strengths and the suggestion here is that rather than choose between them, the way forward lies in identifying the strengths of each position and constructing an eschatology from them.

Each position is able to appeal to strands of biblical teaching for justification. Amillennialism undoubtedly is the strongest position on purely exegetical grounds. The book of Revelation is a series of glimpses behind the scenes of history showing the reality of God's rule beyond the apparent chaos of human experience. That God rules now through Christ despite all appearances to the contrary, is a deeply biblical theme.

Premillennialism, however, bears witness to the fact that God's rule is not just beyond history in an other-worldly sense; it is to be realized in history to the concrete circumstances of human existence. When it expects, therefore, that Christ will come and rule in all the spheres of human life it is echoing the teaching of Jesus, 'Your kingdom come, your will be done on *earth* as it is in heaven' (Mt 6:10). Jesus himself taught: 'I say to you that many will come from the east and the west, and will take their places at the feast with Abraham, Isaac and Jacob in the kingdom of heaven' (Mt 8:11). At the last supper he said: 'I tell you, I will not drink of this fruit of the vine from now on until that day when I drink it anew with you in my Father's kingdom' (Mt 26:29). Jesus anticipated some form of realization of the kingdom of God on earth, in human history, in the resurrection age and this is fitting since history too is God's creation and in his work of redeeming that which is his own, we should expect this to be expressed in the historical arena as in all others. Amillennialism runs the danger of missing this, of conceiving of God's kingdom in Platonic, other-worldly terms. Premillennialism affirms that history too will be redeemed.

Postmillennialism is able to draw upon deep veins of scriptural teaching concerning the turning of the nations to the God of Israel. At certain points of the Old Testament the note of triumphant victory for the people of Israel in the midst of the heathen nations is clearly struck. Isaiah 60 is a prime example of this, as is Zechariah 8:23, 'This is what the Lord Almighty says: "In those days ten men from all languages and nations will take firm hold of one Jew by the edge of his robe and say, 'Let us go with you, because we have heard that God is with you.'"' Isaiah 19:18–25 is a further example: 'In that day five cities in Egypt will speak the language of Canaan and swear allegiance to the Lord Almighty. One of them will be called the City of Destruction. In that day there will be an altar to the Lord in the heart of Egypt, and a monument to the Lord at its border . . . . So the Lord will make himself known to the Egyptians, and in that day they will acknowledge the Lord . . . . They will turn to the Lord, and he will respond to their pleas and heal them . . . . In that day Israel will be the third, along with Egypt and Assyria, a blessing on the earth. The Lord Almighty will bless them, saying, "Blessed be Egypt my people, Assyria my handiwork, and Israel my inheritance."'

What is here portrayed is the conversion of the nations on an immense scale, a worldwide revival that will put all previous revivals in the shade and it is this authentic strand of the biblical witness that postmillennialism is capturing and preserving.

The truth about the future is too big to be contained in any one of the traditional theories; it is to be drawn from them all. In due course we shall return to this theme and endeavour to construct an understanding of the future which does justice to the breadth of the biblical witness. Before doing so, we pause to notice how in the restoration movement of our day the postmillennial hope is receiving a new emphasis after many years of domination by the other points of view.

We have seen how a basic theme for the Anabaptists was that of the fall and restoration of the church. There is an inherent logic which pushes this theme forward. If the church fell from its original vitality but is now in process of recovering that which was lost then it is reasonable to hope both that a restoration might take place and that the church resulting from such a process might surpass anything that has previously been known. It might in fact embark upon a new golden age which will be a prelude to the second coming and will hasten it.

Such themes have been common among restorationist groups. Sometimes the new age has been conceived of as a new Davidic age and, as we have seen, this has been a prominent theme among current movements on the basis of Acts 15:16, 17: 'After this I will return and rebuild David's fallen tent. Its ruins I will rebuild, and I will restore it, that the remnant of men may seek the Lord, and all the Gentiles who bear my name.' Sometimes a 'generation of church life' in which the church will attain to its full maturity is referred to as a prelude to the return of Christ with, of course, the affirmation that 'this is it'.

A further theme, building on a similar foundation, is that of 'the Elijah people'. Jewish anticipation at the time of Jesus was that Elijah would return to herald the coming of the Messiah (Mal 4:5) and that he would do a work of restoration to prepare for him. Jesus saw the fulfilment of this in John the Baptist (Mt 11:14).

It has been a recurrent theme among radical groups that the second coming of Jesus, like his first, will be heralded not by a man but by an Elijah people, by a movement of restoration. Their task will be to prepare for his coming and speed it on his way.

Both these themes coincide with postmillennialism in their expectation that before the second coming the church will enter into a period of universal triumph and therefore the call to the church is: 'Awake, awake, O Zion, clothe yourself with strength. Put on your garments of splendour, O Jerusalem, the holy city. The uncircumcised and defiled will not enter you again. Shake off your dust, rise up, sit enthroned, O Jerusalem. Free yourself from the chains on your neck, O captive Daughter of Zion' (Is 52:1–2).

Applied to today's church these words are seen as a call to enter into the new era of purity and of readiness which is the prelude to the climax of history. Against this backdrop it is easier to understand the call of some for Christians to leave their denominations and join in with the new thing God is doing. The time is short and decision is necessary if the opportunity is not to be missed. It also explains why restoration churches are sometimes referred to as 'new order' churches.

A further remarkable sign that these things are so is discerned by some in the restoration of Israel. It is seen as significant that Israel was restored as a state in its own land in 1947 and that despite overwhelming opposition she has been preserved. Indeed the events which have taken place have been of Old Testament proportions as Israel has been miraculously protected from annihilation. As Paul makes it clear in Romans 9–11 that there is a link between the conversion of the Jews and the final ingathering of souls, could it not be that the restoration of natural Israel and the restoration of spiritual Israel, the church, are parallel events in history heralding the final coming?

For the Puritans, some of whom were the foremost articulators of the postmillennial position, the Jews were of great importance in the scenario which was to accompany the end. It was for this reason that Oliver Cromwell permitted their return to England.

There are many Old Testament prophecies which speak of the return of Israel to the land and, although these referred in the first place to the return from captivity in Babylon, it is argued that these prophecies have a further fulfilment in the end times. Again we see how the Scriptures accompanying the restoration of Israel (the later stages of Isaiah, Ezekiel, Zechariah, Haggai, Ezra and Nehemiah) are seen to have a direct relevance to the church scene of today. These in turn may be related to a further key restoration text, Acts 3:21: 'He must remain in heaven until the time comes for God to restore everything, as he promised long ago through his holy prophets.' The coming of Christ is near and now is the time of restoration!

This understanding of the future makes sense of the claim

by some to be 'the church of the restoration' and also of the rhetoric which appeals to people to shake off the chains of Babylon and to become a part of the church which, in purity, is preparing for the coming of the King and is in fact bringing him back. How are these claims to be evaluated?

What about the future?

We begin our evaluation by returning to the historic debate about the millennium. Each of the millennial positions has its strengths and weaknesses.

Amillennialism is strong in asserting the reign of Christ now beyond history but it runs the danger of devaluing history and suggesting that what really matters is not what is happening on earth but that which is taking place in heaven, in the spiritual sphere. Christian theology has been strongly influenced by Platonic Greek thought with its assertion that earthly things are shadows of realities in the spiritual sphere. This has created a strong other-worldly bias which is in danger of writing-off the earthly and this-worldly spheres, or at best of being unconcerned about them.

Premillennialism avoids this by seeing that the totality of human experience must become the arena for God's kingdom and that therefore one day, after Christ's coming, all things will be restored according to God's will in a great millennial sabbath. The weakness of this view is that it postpones the fulfilment of hope and expectation until after the coming of Christ and can therefore be pessimistic about anything that is likely to happen until that time. There is hope for the world, but not much for what remains of human history. The earth faces catastrophe, war and spiritual decline until the coming of Christ. The church's concern until then is simply to hang on and to endure to the end, but not to attempt great enterprises in the confidence that there will be success.

Postmillennialism is far more optimistic. The coming of Christ is anticipated as the climax of history, but before that there is a last ingathering to be expected and to be worked for as God demonstrates his power through the church. Ephesians makes it plain that God has a universal, cosmic purpose to restore the world and in anticipation of that he is demonstrating his wisdom now through the church: 'His intent was that now, through the church, the manifold wisdom of God should be made known to the rulers and authorities in the heavenly realms, according to his eternal purpose which he accomplished in Christ Jesus our Lord' (Eph 3:10–11).

God's power and wisdom are demonstrated in taking those who are weak and foolish and in revealing himself to and through them. Therefore before Christ comes and history is fulfilled God will manifest himself through the church in a way which is plain for all to see and he will be glorified before the rulers and authorities.

If postmillennialism has a weakness it is that it could optimistically overdraw and overdefine what is possible this side of Christ's coming. Whatever is achieved in history, there is that which can only be achieved at Christ's coming; and whatever is achieved then will not be credited to man, as if he had brought it to pass, but to God. Postmillennialism is not optimism about human nature but faith in the God who is all-powerful and who demonstrates his sovereignty, as he did at the cross, by taking that which is the weakest and the worst and making it into the finest and best.

If we draw out the strong points in these positions we are left with a theology that affirms the rule of God now over this age and this world, and which expects at Christ's coming a reclaiming of all that has been alienated from God so that in space and time the kingdom of God is fully realized. Such a theology maintains that, even before that day, it is God's purpose to gather in the nations and to be gracious to them in history through the gospel so that there is everything to hope and work for *now* as well as in the beyond. This theology affirms the future in every conceivable way but not apart from God and his activity. Without him there is no hope. With him there is everything to hope for in time and in eternity.

What about Israel?

Not all restoration groups make much of Israel, but some do, so it is important to investigate Israel's place in the future scheme. Many passages in the Old Testament could be pressed into service to interpret Israel, but the passage around which all must hinge is a New Testament one, Romans 9–11, where Paul deals specifically with the future of natural Israel.

It is significant that this passage follows on immediately from Romans 8:37–39 where Paul affirms that nothing can separate us from the love of God. It is in illustration of this theme that Paul discusses the fate of Israel. What hope is there for them now that they have rejected the Messiah?

(1) He asserts that Israel has failed to inherit God's promises because of unbelief (9:30–33). The result of their rejection is that the Gentiles have been included through faith in those same promises. Blessing for the Gentiles is therefore the result of Israel's unbelief and disobedience.

(2) Israel's fall is not final, because God's rejection is not final. He remains true to his purposes of election (11:28–29) and will not be deflected. For the sake of his promises to the patriarchs God will be merciful to Israel when they cease their unbelief (11:23). They have been given over to disobedience in order that God might show them mercy (11: 31–32).

(3) All Israel, meaning the bulk of the people rather than every single one of them, will at some future time be saved and the means of this will be the mercy which they see among the Gentiles. What they see in the Gentiles will provoke them to jealousy (11:13–14, 31) and they themselves will desire it and will be grafted back into God's purpose. This will take place when the gospel has had its impact among the Gentiles (11:25).

(4) The result of this will be even greater blessing for the world. If the Jews' rejection of the gospel meant life for the Gentiles, their conversion has even greater prospects in store. 'For if their rejection is the reconciliation of the world, what will their acceptance be but life from the dead?' (Rom 11:15). Surely Paul intends us to understand here that the conversion of the Jews will be accompanied by the communication of life to the nations on a universal and unprecedented scale.

So there is a future in the purposes of God for the people of Israel. But here we must be careful what conclusions we draw. For many Christians the current state of Israel is the fulfilment of prophecy. There is a form of Christian Zionism which makes claims for the state of Israel which it has no right to make. So we are told that Israel still enjoys 'most favoured nation' status with God. Because God said to Abraham, 'I will bless those who bless you' (Gen 12:3) and because natural Israel is still to be regarded as the 'apple of his eye' (Deut 32:10), how we respond to Israel is treated as a touchstone of spirituality. Anybody who loves God should and must support Israel wholeheartedly! This extends to governments. The history of foreign policy is interpreted to prove that those who have supported Israel have been blessed by God. Arthur Balfour, Winston Churchill and Harold Wilson are all examples of men whom God honoured because they honoured Israel!

More worrying than these assertions is the belief that to help Israel militarily is a virtuous act and the tendency to turn a blind eye to violations of human rights. There is no doubt that in the present state of Israel there are strong elements of secularism and of racism. There can also be no doubt that the Palestinian Arabs displaced from their land by the Jews have a legitimate right to some form of consideration. To ignore these things and to believe that because the Jews are the chosen people their interests take precedence over all others is not a Christian position. It is a form of nationalism that is a denial of the new people and the new creation which is coming to be in Christ.

The fact is that, in biblical terms, there is no significance in the founding of the Jewish state as such. What is of importance, however, is that throughout history the Jewish *people* have been preserved despite all forms of persecution and anti-Semitism. The return to Israel demonstrates and highlights this fact and in it we may see the hand of God. But the Jewish people remain as sinful as any other people and are as much under judgement as us all. God does not approve of them, but his grace is not based upon approval. It is his purpose to maintain Israel as a people in order that the time may come when his ancient promises and covenants may be fulfilled and he may show mercy to them. The significance of Romans 9–11 is not that God favours Israel above all other nations but that in the favour God is showing in Christ to every nation, Israel will not finally be excluded but will come to share in his benefits.

It is not certain in what Paul says whether the conversion of the Jews is to be seen as the *means* whereby 'life from the dead' will come to the world or simply as its accompaniment, but there is reason to believe that the acceptance of Israel will indeed be instrumental in the worldwide revival which precedes Christ's coming. It may be speculative to say so, but it could be that the conversion of the Jews will be the point of breaking through into the Islamic world which has so far been so resistant to Christ. It would take a miracle for this to happen, but miracles are possible in the economy of God. It has been said that the candle of the Gentiles was lit from the candle of the Jews in order that in due course the candle of the Jews may be lit again from that of the Gentiles so that both may burn powerfully together. This is a vivid hope and contributes to the expectation—which is firmly based in Scripture—of a restoration of the church among Jews and Gentiles for the blessing of the world before the day of the Lord arrives.

What about the church?

If these things are so then in the coming of the Lord there is the greatest hope possible, but there is an exciting possibility to be reckoned with even before that. The greatest age of the church has yet to come. In the visionary portrayal of Christ's coming in Revelation 19, verse 7 reads: 'Let us rejoice and be glad and give him glory! For the wedding of the Lamb has come, and his bride has made herself ready.' The expectation of John was that the Christ would be coming for a bride prepared and ready for him, that the bride would have made herself ready for her Lord. Since the church in her present condition can hardly be described in this way, this suggests that there is yet work to do. Of most significance in this regard is the prayer of Jesus in John 17: 20–23: 'My prayer is not for them alone. I pray also for those who will believe in me through their message, that all of them may be one, Father, just as you are in me and I am in you. May they also be in us so that the world may believe that you have sent me. I have given them the glory that you gave me, that they may be one as we are one: I in them and you in me. May they be brought to complete unity to let the world know that you sent me and have loved them even as you have loved me.' This prayer has not yet been fulfilled. It is reasonable to expect that the prayer of Jesus will be answered and it was clearly intended to be fulfilled in history as a witness to an unbelieving world.

How will it be fulfilled? Only by the power of God in response to the desires of our hearts. It is beyond the ability of man to engineer the visible unity of the church. Ecumenism is right in its instincts but wrong in its methods. Equally, exponents of restoration who may imagine that they have found the formula are mistaken. The unity of the church will only be brought to pass by the power of God and even he appears to have a difficult job on, given the years of division, disagreement and disobedience which have passed! But the purposes of God ripen fast. When God moves he is able to do in a moment what man has been attempting for centuries. It is precisely such a work of God for which we should be praying, waiting upon God for it to come to pass.

What will the result be for the church?

The church will be one

Jesus prayed for the visible unity of the church. This does not mean that the church needs to be a monolothic, uniform whole, but that the immense and rich variety which already characterizes the church will be interpenetrated with a unity, a oneness, a trust and a coherence which will be evident and which will speak of Christ. Those differing insights of which separate parts of the church are stewards will be surrendered and received by the whole with gratitude. Variant forms of worship will be appreciated for their strengths and not rejected because of their weaknesses. From their historic experiences the various families of the church will be able to contribute to the common wealth. Nothing which is good will be lost or forgotten. Mutual enrichment will be the order of the day.

The church will be holy

Since the church belongs exclusively to God there is no room for unholy resistance to him among his people. Resistance to God must fall away and unholiness must be cauterized. Reformation of abuses and errors will take place among all groups of God's people since none is complete. The church will become substantially whole and holy and will correct those who fall with gentleness and righteousness. It will be evident that the church is God's church, the dwelling place of the Living and Holy One.

The church will be catholic

It is God's declared purpose to gather a people from the whole earth and to have expressed in his church the variety of language, cultures and peoples that the earth has brought forth. In all cultures and ethnic groups there will be those who are recognizably Christ's and are at one with the universal church in a way that transcends the multitude of divisions which sin has produced. The church will be a genuinely international and supranational people who have broken free from the limiting and parochial nationalism that is much in evidence today. This new nation among the nations will be in a position to challenge the ancient hostilities of the earth's power groups and to make for peace.

The church will be apostolic

The doctrine and teachings of the church will be derived from the apostolic witness. False doctrines will be reformed and inadequate teaching filled out. It will be manifest that what is taught and proclaimed now is the same word as the apostles proclaimed and that the apostolic task of being sent out with the good news is being fulfilled now through the contemporary church.

For many such a vision of the church will seem hopelessly idealistic, but it is simply the vision brought to fulfilment of one, holy, catholic and apostolic church in which God's people have confessed their faith through the ages. It is a biblical and a worthy vision which offers hope for the world, hope for the church, hope for human society and hope for the future. It is a vision which motivates us to committed living within the church and to concerned witness among the affairs of men. It will contain unexpected elements and be brought to pass in ways of which now we can scarcely conceive. It is unwise to narrow down our expectations, lest like the Pharisees we miss the fulfilling of prophecy before our very eyes because we are caught up in bigotry. But ultimately it is the vision of restoration.

> It was he who gave some to be apostles, some to be prophets, some to be evangelists, and some to be pastors and teachers, to prepare God's people for works of service, so that the body of Christ may be built up until we all reach unity in the faith and in the knowledge of the Son of God and become mature, attaining to the whole measure of the fulness of Christ.

Then we will no longer be infants, tossed back and forth by the waves, and blown here and there by every wind of teaching and by the cunning and craftiness of men in their deceitful scheming. Instead, speaking the truth in love, we will in all things grow up into him who is the Head, that is Christ. From him the whole body, jointed and held together by every supporting ligament, grows and builds itself up in love, as each part does its work.

Ephesians 4:11–16

Further Reading

Berkhof, Hendrik, *Christ and the Powers* (Herald Press 1962).

Durnbaugh, Donald F., *The Believers' Church* (Macmillan 1968).

Dyck, Cornelius J. (ed.), *An Introduction to Mennonite History* (Herald Press 1967).

Estep, William R., *The Anabaptists* (Eerdmans 1975).

Foster, Richard J., *Celebration of Discipline* (Hodder and Stoughton 1980).

Gish, Art, *Living in Christian Community* (Herald Press 1979).

Jeschke, Marlin, *Discipling the Brother* (Herald Press 1972).

Littel, Franklin H., *The Origins of Sectarian Protestantism* (Macmillan 1964).

Lovelace, Richard, *Dynamics of Spiritual Life* (Paternoster Press 1979).

Murray, Iain H., *The Puritan Hope* (Banner of Truth 1971).

Packer, James I., *Keep in Step with the Spirit* (Inter-Varsity Press 1984).

Richards, Lawrence O., *A New Face for the Church* (Zondervan 1970).

Richards, Lawrence O., and Hoeldtke, Clyde, *Theology of Church Leadership* (Zondervan 1980).

Sider, Ronald J., *Christ and Violence* (Lion Publishing 1980).

Snyder, Howard A., *The Community of the King* (Inter-Varsity Press 1977).
Snyder, Howard A., *New Wineskins* (Marshall, Morgan and Scott 1977).
Snyder, Howard A., *Liberating the Church* (Marshalls 1983).
Sugden, Christopher, *Radical Discipleship* (Marshall, Morgan and Scott 1981).
Trudinger, Ron, *Built to Last* (Kingsway Publications 1982).
Verduin, Leonard, *The Reformers and Their Stepchildren* (Paternoster Press 1964).
Wallis, Arthur, *The Radical Christian* (Kingsway Publications 1981).
Wallis, Jim B., *Agenda for Biblical People* (Harper and Row 1976).
Wallis, Jim B., *The Call to Conversion* (Lion Publishing 1982).
Williams, George H., *The Radical Reformation* (Westminster Press 1962).
Yoder, John Howard, *The Politics of Jesus* (Eerdmans 1972).

Restoration in the Church

by Terry Virgo

God is restoring his church. Many are now seeing the need to apply New Testament principles to their church structures and time-honoured traditions. Flexibility and freedom are on the increase.

This book takes an inside look at what has been called 'the house church movement' and reveals how amazing growth has come from a rediscovery of Scripture's teaching on ministries in the church. Whatever our situation, we will find a fresh challenge in what the author has to say.

☐ The traditional evangelical is reminded that restoration is rooted in the orthodox teaching of the Reformers.

☐ The charismatic is asked not to stop with personal gifts but to go on to embrace the ministries of apostle and prophet.

☐ Those already committed to restoration are urged to be watchful, avoiding complacency and ready to move on to whatever God has in store.

Terry Virgo is based at Clarendon Church, Hove, Brighton. A frequent visitor to many countries with the message of restoration, he is highly respected for his ministry to church leaders in various denominations, and is a popular speaker at Bible Weeks each year. He is married with five children.

k *Kingsway Publications*

The Radical Christian

by Arthur Wallis

God's Holy Spirit is at work to change us into the likeness of Christ. Do we realize what a radical change this means?

This book challenges us to re-examine some of our cherished customs and beliefs. It shows how Scripture can guide us over such issues as church unity, water and Spirit baptism, and denominational loyalty.

The author confesses that this has not been an easy book to write. Nor will it be easy for us to receive. It calls for a verdict on God's truth—and so for a verdict on ourselves. Each one of us must decide: am I a compromiser, or a radical?

The axe is laid to the root of the tree.